REGENTS RENAISSANCE DRAMA SERIES

General Editor: Cyrus Hoy
Advisory Editor: G. E. Bentley

PERKIN WARBECK

JOHN FORD

Perkin Warbeck

Edited by

DONALD K. ANDERSON, JR.

UNIVERSITY OF NEBRASKA PRESS · LINCOLN

Regents Renaissance Drama Series

The purpose of the Regents Renaissance Drama Series is to provide soundly edited texts, in modern spelling, of the more significant plays of the Elizabethan, Jacobean, and Caroline theater. Each text in the series is based on a fresh collation of all sixteenth- and seventeenth-century editions. The textual notes, which appear above the line at the bottom of each page, record all substantive departures from the edition used as the copy-text. Variant substantive readings among sixteenth- and seventeenth-century editions are listed there as well. In cases where two or more of the old editions present widely divergent readings, a list of substantive variants in editions through the seventeenth century is given in an appendix. Editions after 1700 are referred to in the textual notes only when an emendation originating in some one of them is received into the text. Variants of accidentals (spelling, punctuation, capitalization) are not recorded in the notes. Contracted forms of characters' names are silently expanded in speech prefixes and stage directions, and, in the case of speech prefixes, are regularized. Additions to the stage directions of the copy-text are enclosed in brackets. Stage directions such as "within" or "aside" are enclosed in parentheses when they occur in the copy-text.

Spelling has been modernized along consciously conservative lines. "Murther" has become "murder," and "burthen," "burden," but within the limits of a modernized text, and with the following exceptions, the linguistic quality of the original has been carefully preserved. The variety of contracted forms (*'em, 'am, 'm, 'um, 'hem*) used in the drama of the period for the pronoun *them* are here regularly given as *'em*, and the alternation between *a'th'* and *o'th'* (for *on* or *of the*) is regularly reproduced as *o'th'*. The copy-text distinction between preterite endings in *-d* and *-ed* is preserved except where the elision of *e* occurs in the penultimate syllable; in such cases, the final syllable is contracted. Thus, where the old editions read "threat'ned," those of the present series read "threaten'd." Where, in the old editions, a contracted preterite in *-y'd* would yield *-i'd* in modern spelling (as in "try'd," "cry'd," "deny'd"), the word is here given in its full form (e.g., "tried," "cried," "denied").

Punctuation has been brought into accord with modern practices. The effort here has been to achieve a balance between the generally light pointing of the old editions, and a system of punctuation which, without overloading the text with exclamation marks, semicolons, and dashes, will make the often loosely flowing verse (and prose) of the original syntactically intelligible to the modern reader. Dashes are regularly used only to indicate interrupted speeches, or shifts of address within a single speech.

Explanatory notes, chiefly concerned with glossing obsolete words and phrases, are printed below the textual notes at the bottom of each page. References to stage directions in the notes follow the admirable system of the Revels editions, whereby stage directions are keyed, decimally, to the line of the text before or after which they occur. Thus, a note on 0.2 has reference to the second line of the stage direction at the beginning of the scene in question. A note on 115.1 has reference to the first line of the stage direction following line 115 of the text of the relevant scene.

CYRUS HOY

University of Rochester

Contents

Abbreviations

Bacon
: Francis Bacon. *History of the Reign of King Henry VII*, 1622. James Spedding, Robert L. Ellis, and Douglas D. Heath, eds. *The Works of Francis Bacon.* 11 vols. Boston, 1857–1864.

Baskervill
: Charles R. Baskervill, Virgil B. Heltzel, and Arthur H. Nethercot, eds. *Elizabethan and Stuart Plays.* New York, 1934.

Coleridge
: Hartley Coleridge, ed. *The Dramatic Works of Massinger and Ford.* London, 1869 (first published in 1840).

corr.
: corrected

Dyce
: Alexander Dyce and William Gifford, eds. *The Works of John Ford.* 3 vols. London, 1869 (contains Dyce's additions to Gifford's edition of 1827).

Ellis
: Havelock Ellis, ed. *John Ford.* The Mermaid Series. London, 1888.

Gainsford
: Thomas Gainsford. *True and Wonderful History of Perkin Warbeck*, 1618. In appendix to Struble's *Perkin Warbeck;* see Struble, below.

Gifford
: See Dyce, above.

OED
: *Oxford English Dictionary*

Q
: 1634 quarto of *Perkin Warbeck*

S.D.
: stage direction

S.P.
: speech prefix

Struble
: Mildred C. Struble, ed. *A Critical Edition of Ford's Perkin Warbeck.* Seattle, 1926.

Sugden
: E. H. Sugden. *A Topographical Dictionary to the Works of Shakespeare and His Fellow Dramatists.* Manchester, 1925.

Tilley
: Morris Palmer Tilley. *A Dictionary of the Proverbs in England in the Sixteenth and Seventeenth Centuries.* Ann Arbor, 1950.

uncorr.   uncorrected

Weber   Henry Weber, ed. *The Dramatic Works of John Ford.* 2 vols.
            Edinburgh, 1811.

1714   Ed. anonymous. *The Chronicle History of Perkin Warbeck.*
            London, 1714.

Introduction

John Ford's *The Chronicle History of Perkin Warbeck, A Strange Truth*, was first printed in 1634, having been listed in the Stationers' Register on February 24 of the same year. When it was written or first staged is not known; the phrase "acted (some-times)" on the title page might mean that the play had been performed well before its printing.[1] Ford could not have written it before 1622, the publication date of one of his principal sources, Bacon's *History of the Reign of King Henry VII*. This, with Thomas Gainsford's *True and Wonderful History of Perkin Warbeck* (1618), provided Ford with the major materials of his drama. Many lines in the play are quite similar to passages in one or the other of these works, and Ford's acknowledgment, in his dedication, of some indebtedness to "a late both learned and an honourable pen" is very likely a reference to Bacon. As for the verbal parallels (see explanatory notes), Ford seems to borrow from the two histories about equally: more from Bacon in Acts II and V, more from Gainsford in Acts III and IV, and about the same from both in Act I. Six of the eighteen scenes show no such use of the sources. For one of the six, King James's giving of Katherine to Warbeck (II.iii), Ford has at his disposal Gainsford's expanded and euphuistic account of Warbeck's wooing of Katherine, but rejects it; if any character speaks in Gainsford's style, it is Daliell (I.ii), Katherine's ill-fated suitor, whose stilted phrases are ridiculed by Katherine's father, the Earl of Huntley.

Taking his plot from the two histories, Ford adds to, omits from, and alters their accounts very effectively. In his emphasis, he follows Bacon more closely than he does Gainsford, especially in portraying Henry VII. Bacon surpasses all other chroniclers in his analysis of the king's character, and most of his conclusions are complimentary. Ford is even more favorable, often changing the sequence of historical events to enhance Henry's foresight. Gainsford pays scant attention to personality and motives.

For an adequate appreciation of the play, some knowledge of the

[1] This possibility is discussed by Gerald E. Bentley in his *The Jacobean and Caroline Stage* (Oxford, 1941–1956), III, 455–456.

historical Warbeck is helpful. Henry VII ruled England from 1485 to 1509; nothing better illustrates both the difficulties besetting him and the effectiveness with which he handled them than the Warbeck episode. From 1491 until 1499, the year he was executed, Warbeck claimed that he was Richard, Duke of York, second son of Edward IV, and hence the rightful king of England. Actually, according to general belief then and now, both sons of Edward had been murdered in the Tower during the reign of their uncle, Richard III. But during Henry's reign disaffected Yorkists in both England and Ireland were ready to support any rival to the king, who had slain the Yorkist Richard III at Bosworth Field and claimed the throne as a Lancastrian (that is, as a descendant of John of Gaunt, Duke of Lancaster); even though Henry subsequently married Elizabeth, daughter of Edward IV, and thus joined the two factious houses, Yorkist opposition persisted.

Warbeck was not the only pretender to the throne: both Lambert Simnel in 1487 and Rafe Wilford in 1499 claimed they were Edward, Earl of Warwick, a nephew of Edward IV. However, the real Earl of Warwick was imprisoned in the Tower, from which he sought to flee with Warbeck in 1499 only to be apprehended and hanged with the impostor. Simnel confessed that he was a counterfeit, and was pardoned by Henry; Wilford was hanged. But Warbeck, although he eventually confessed publicly from the scaffold his imposture and his humble ancestry, caused Henry much more trouble.

Perkin Warbeck was born in Tournay, Flanders; his parents were John Osbeck, controller of the town, and Catherine de Faro. Nothing of importance is known about his activities until 1491, when, a young man, he sailed to Cork, Ireland. Here his regal bearing and language (having been acquired, very likely, under the tutelage of Margaret of Burgundy, sister of Edward IV) were so imposing that he was thought to be of noble birth. When asked if he was the Earl of Warwick, an illegitimate son of Richard III, or Richard, Duke of York, he denied the first two identities but claimed the third one. In the following year Charles VIII invited the "duke" to his court; however, a treaty between Charles and Henry resulted in Warbeck's leaving France for Flanders, where he was cordially received by Margaret as her nephew. When Henry, in retaliation, terminated trade with Flanders, Warbeck moved to Vienna and the Emperor Maximilian. In the meantime, more Yorkists had become involved with Warbeck; Henry, aware of the peril, sent spies to Flanders, who there persuaded two prominent English supporters of the pretender,

Sir Robert Clifford and William Barley, to defect. Upon his return, Clifford confessed and was pardoned; he also disclosed to Henry the names of many Englishmen associated with Warbeck. Foremost among these was the king's lord chamberlain, Sir William Stanley, who had been of great help in obtaining him the crown. As a result, Stanley, having admitted his guilt, was executed in 1495.

Later in the same year, Warbeck made an unsuccessful landing in Kent, met with an apathetic response in Ireland, and then went to Scotland, where he was warmly received by James IV. James accepted him as the son of Edward IV and effected his marriage with Lady Katherine Gordon, a relative of the Scottish king. James also supported Warbeck militarily, making an incursion into English territory; the venture proved fruitless, however, for Englishmen failed to flock around the banner of the "Duke of York." To meet this peril, Henry levied subsidies. One result was that the Cornish, resenting the additional taxes, rebelled; they marched on London, but were routed at Blackheath by Henry's forces. Encouraged by the uprising, James and Warbeck made a second incursion, which was no more successful than the first one.

Meanwhile, Hialas, an emissary from King Ferdinand of Spain, visited Henry and urged him to initiate peace with James. The English king did so, and in 1497 a treaty resulted. One consequence was the departure of Warbeck and Katherine to Ireland. In September of the same year Warbeck, learning of further discontent among the Cornish, landed in Cornwall, rounded up some followers, and besieged Exeter. But his forces were defeated and soon he was captured, having surrendered himself from sanctuary in a Hampshire monastery on the condition that he not be executed. By Henry's order he was taken to London, led through the streets, and put into prison. In 1499 he escaped, but was recaptured, displayed in the stocks, and made to read a public confession. He then was moved to the Tower, where the Earl of Warwick already was imprisoned. Shortly thereafter he arranged an escape for both himself and the earl, but the plan was discovered and both men were promptly condemned and executed. Katherine, having been taken by Henry's forces when Warbeck was defeated in 1497, was graciously received by the king, who bestowed upon her pensions and land grants. She spent the remainder of her life (she died in 1537) at the English court, where she married three more times.

T. S. Eliot has called *Perkin Warbeck* "unquestionably Ford's highest achievement, and . . . one of the very best historical plays outside of Shakespeare in the whole of Elizabethan and Jacobean drama."[2] Some twentieth-century commentators disagree with the first part of Eliot's statement, asserting that of the seven extant plays solely and unquestionably Ford's, either *The Broken Heart* or *'Tis Pity She's a Whore* is the best; but there has been no quarrel about the stature of *Perkin Warbeck* as a historical drama. Written several decades after Shakespeare's chronicle plays, it easily surpasses its contemporaries in that genre. In a sense, it is a continuation of Shakespeare's history of England, since Ford tells what happened after Richard III was defeated by the Earl of Richmond (Henry VII) at Bosworth Field in 1485. The dramas of the earlier playwright must have been familiar to the later one; indeed, *Richard II* contains a likely source (III.ii) for one of Ford's scenes: the landing of Warbeck on the coast of Cornwall (IV.v). At the same time, *Perkin Warbeck* is much more than a supplement to Shakespeare; Ford not only presents a different political philosophy (more akin to that of Machiavelli and Bacon) but also underscores a steadfast devotion between an ennobled Warbeck and his wife, Katherine, that is like his treatment of love in his other plays (none of which are chronicles). In the play, Warbeck is to be admired in his personal relationships but condemned for his politics. That Ford is able to resolve the paradox of triumph and failure testifies to his skill as a playwright.

Ford presents Warbeck sympathetically (Bacon, Gainsford, and the other chroniclers did just the opposite), yet leaves no doubt that he is an impostor. The latter point of view was mandatory, for if the playwright had implied that Warbeck was indeed the son of Edward IV he would have been challenging the succession of the Stuarts, not to mention that of the Tudors; James I had become king of England in 1603 because he was a descendant of James IV of Scotland and his wife, Margaret, daughter of Henry VII. Ford handles the problem of characterization by several means. One is to keep Warbeck off the stage until Act II, by which time Henry and his counselors have fully described the imposture to the audience. Another is to make all of the Scottish characters, with the exception of James IV, skeptical of Warbeck's claims; even Katherine, though constant to her husband, expresses some doubt. Still another device is to portray Warbeck's advisers (the Mayor of Cork, Heron, Astley, and Sketon) as comical, inept opportunists. Thus, although Warbeck himself never admits

[2] T. S. Eliot, *Selected Essays 1917–1932* (New York, 1932), p. 177.

that he is a counterfeit (whereas all the chronicles cite his public confession), Ford unquestionably presents him as one.

If this be so, why is Warbeck such an impressive figure in the play? Here again Ford manipulates his material with skill. He portrays Warbeck as utterly convinced of his royal birth. The protagonist speaks no soliloquies; he reveals no inner conflict. Instead, the main tension of the play is that between him (and his wife) and fate. His lofty language and aspirations may seem presumptuous when he first appears, as a claimant at the court of James. But they become more and more impressive as he undergoes dismissal, imprisonment, and execution, and when, in the stocks, he voices his love for Katherine. A similar emphasis upon "resolution" is found in *The Golden Meane* (1613), a prose pamphlet generally attributed to Ford, which explains that a truly noble person will persevere in spite of banishment, prison, or death; and one commentator, Clifford Leech, sees Warbeck as "a Fordian aristocrat, dignified by his own steadfastness in delusion."[3] Analyzing *Perkin Warbeck*, one might argue that its titular character is a madman, possessed with illusions of royalty. Urswick, one of Henry's aides, makes this very diagnosis; but it comes in the final act, long after Warbeck has made his full impact upon the other characters and, presumably, the audience. Of paramount importance is Ford's poetic power: when Warbeck is expressing courage, love, or defiance, he is no counterfeit, and his utterances are moving; their brilliance blinds us, at least for the moment, to the shadows surrounding him.

While Warbeck is the play's central figure, he is not the leading exponent of its political doctrine. That role Ford reserves for Henry VII, whom he idealizes as a master of kingship. As in the case of Warbeck, the playwright treats Henry more favorably than did any of the chroniclers. All of the latter were sympathetic, but they qualified their praise. Bacon, for example, saw some avarice in the king's collecting of subsidies, and Gainsford some confusion in his handling of the Cornish revolt; in *Perkin Warbeck*, he is flawless. Sometimes Ford alters history to increase Henry's statecraft. For example, the playwright places before instead of after the first Scottish incursion Henry's conference with Hialas (the Spanish emissary) in which a peace treaty between England and Scotland is planned; therefore, when in the next scene (III.iv) James and Warbeck lead on their marauding

[3] Clifford Leech, *John Ford and the Drama of His Time* (London, 1957), p. 92.

forces, their efforts seem shortsighted and futile. Another instance occurs in the fourth scene of Act IV, when Henry, anticipating Warbeck's attack on Exeter even before he has landed in Cornwall, sends his forces to Salisbury (located midway between Exeter and London); in the accounts of both Bacon and Gainsford, Henry shows no foresight concerning Exeter, and when it is besieged his troops are near London, not in Salisbury.

Also noteworthy is Ford's emphasis on Henry's pragmatism: the king often stresses the importance of money, believing that money increases loyalty and manpower; he expertly utilizes his counselors (in contrast to James and to Warbeck), and on one occasion defers to their advice; he ably delegates authority to his subordinates; he skillfully metes out justice, whether it be mercy or punishment. For this concept of the ideal ruler, the playwright probably is indebted to the many treatises *de regimine principum* ("the conduct of princes"), especially to those of the more realistic theorists such as Machiavelli and Bacon. A more direct proof of Ford's interest in kingship appears in his pamphlet *A Line of Life*. Published in 1620, the prose work describes the able ruler as a statesman and a promoter of international peace, and it cites James I of England as an example of such a king. *Perkin Warbeck*'s Henry VII would seem to be another one.

In Ford's depiction of kingship, Warbeck and James are contrasted to Henry. Although the play should not be read as an attack upon the theory of the divine right of kings (Henry himself supports it on several occasions), it does stress the importance of the *de facto* basis of sovereignty. Henry, while he may be God's appointed deputy, sees to it that his troops are well armed and well paid. Warbeck, on the other hand, relies entirely on the *de jure* basis of sovereignty, contending that his birthright entitles him to the throne. This argument at first impresses James and induces him to support Warbeck, but after several expensive raids into English territory have led to no rebellion and after Henry has offered an attractive truce, James assumes an attitude like that of Henry, and dismisses Warbeck. Warbeck fails politically not because he is an impostor but because he is impractical and is encountering a much more competent adversary. When he lands in Cornwall for his final and futile invasion of England, he calls upon "horrors," "fear," and "numbness" to strike Henry's forces, and he depends greatly on his "divinity of royal birth." Henry relies on the more tangible assets of money, manpower, and treaty, and the outcome of the conflict is never in doubt.

It should be noted that Ford, in his treatment of the Warbeck story, makes a confession by the pretender unnecessary. As previously explained, by the time Warbeck first appears (II.i), Henry and his counselors already have thoroughly described his imposture; in addition, because Ford, as the play progresses, resolves the conflict between Warbeck and Henry in terms of political skill rather than hereditary right, the question of Warbeck's identity never reappears to demand further consideration. Whether he is a blue-blooded Plantagenet or a pathological liar is beside the point; he dies because Henry time and again has outmaneuvered him. Hence there is no dramatic necessity for a final public confession by Warbeck, and Ford is free to present him as an individual who is invariably eloquent, courageous, and sincere, albeit disastrously impractical.

Finally, something must be said about the rich variety of characterization and language in *Perkin Warbeck*. Ford's portrayals of the Mayor of Cork, Huntley, Henry, and Warbeck provide ample evidence, though that of Katherine could also be cited. John a Water, the Mayor of Cork, is the most comical character in the play. As one of Warbeck's counselors (all of whom are ludicrous except Frion), this petty politician is so steeped in equivocation that, even when discussing a dance, he cannot make an unqualified statement:

> Surely there is, if I be not deceived, a kind of gravity in merriment; as there is, or perhaps ought to be, respect of persons in the quality of carriage, which is, as it is construed, either so, or so. (II.iii.170–173)

The Earl of Huntley, Katherine's father, adds vigor and warmth to the drama. For example, at the wedding feast for Warbeck and his daughter, he speaks to Daliell with the bitter irony of a malcontent—and a brokenhearted father:

> Pish, then I see
> Thou dost not know the flexible condition
> Of my apt nature. I can laugh, laugh heartily
> When the gout cramps my joints; let but the stone
> Stop in my bladder, I am straight a-singing;
> The quartan-fever shrinking every limb
> Sets me a-cap'ring straight. Do but betray me,
> And bind me a friend ever. What! I trust
> The losing of a daughter (though I doted
> On every hair that grew to trim her head)
> Admits not any pain like one of these.
> (III.ii.31–41)

Henry VII speaks in still another tongue. His language is that of the treatises *de regimine principum*, hundreds of which had been written about the all-important conduct of kings. Shortly before Warbeck's capture, for instance, Henry describes to his lords, in an obvious reference to James IV's contrasting practices, his conscientious and prudent financial policies:

> Such voluntary favors as our people
> In duty aid us with, we never scatter'd
> On cobweb parasites, or lavish'd out
> In riot or a needless hospitality.
> No undeserving favorite doth boast
> His issues from our treasury; our charge
> Flows through all Europe, proving us but steward
> Of every contribution, which provides
> Against the creeping canker of disturbance.
>
> (IV.iv.46–54)

Thus Ford's idealization of Henry is found in the latter's language as well as in his actions.

But it is Perkin Warbeck who dominates the play. The humorous equivocations of the Mayor, the biting sarcasms of Huntley, the sage aphorisms of Henry—all are secondary to the regal eloquence of Warbeck. In lines charged with metaphor and simile, he speaks the language of a king, or (more accurately) the language to which any king should aspire. That fact is clearly established in his first appearance (II.i): having been ceremoniously introduced to King James, Warbeck for forty uninterrupted lines proclaims his identity as the Duke of York; James then speaks five lines, after which Warbeck continues for eighteen more. At this point, James says to him: "He must be more than subject, who can utter/ The language of a king, and such is thine." Warbeck's impressive diction continues to the end of the play, whether he be speaking tenderly to his wife, exhorting his followers to battle, berating Lambert Simnel, defying Henry, or facing death. Two short passages will illustrate Perkin's eloquence. On the eve of his first incursion into England, he bids farewell to Katherine:

> Now dearest, ere sweet sleep shall seal those eyes,
> Love's precious tapers, give me leave to use
> A parting ceremony; for tomorrow
> It would be sacrilege to intrude upon

The temple of thy peace. Swift as the morning
Must I break from the down of thy embraces
To put on steel and trace the paths which lead
Through various hazards to a careful throne.
(III.ii.139–146)

Later in the play, when he is urged by Simnel to confess imposture
and seek pardon from Henry, Warbeck's scorn is overpowering:

For pardon? Hold, my heartstrings, whiles contempt
Of injuries in scorn may bid defiance
To this base man's foul language.—Thou poor vermin,
How dar'st thou creep so near me? Thou an earl?
Why, thou enjoy'st as much of happiness
As all the swinge of slight ambition flew at.
A dunghill was thy cradle. So a puddle
By virtue of the sunbeams breathes a vapor
To infect the purer air, which drops again
Into the muddy womb that first exhal'd it.
(V.iii.53–62)

None of the play's sources mention such a speech. Nor do they record
any conversation, not to mention confrontation, between Warbeck
and Henry such as that in Act V. And instead of publicly confessing
his guilt, Ford's undaunted "Richard IV" makes a magnificent final
exit as he and his counselors go to their execution. Surely Dawbney,
Henry's lord chamberlain, pays tribute to the playwright as well as
to the pretender when he exclaims, as Perkin leaves for his death:
". . . impostor beyond precedent!/ No chronicle records his fellow."

THE TEXT

Perkin Warbeck was entered in the Stationers' Register on February
24, 1633/34:

Hugh Beeston. Entred for his Copy under the hands of Sir
Henry Herbert and Master Aspley warden (observing the
Caution in the License) a Tragedy called PERKIN WAR-
BECKE by JOHN FFORD.[4]

4 See *A Transcript of the Registers of the Company of Stationers of London:
1554–1640 A.D.*, ed. Edward Arber (London, 1875–1894), IV. 288.

In 1634 the play was printed for Beeston by "T. P." On the title page of the quarto appear Ford's Latin anagram, *Fide Honor*, and the statement "Acted (some-times) by the Queenes Maiesties Servants at the Phoenix in Drurie lane." The text is preceded by Ford's dedicatory epistle to the Earl of Newcastle and by five commendatory poems written by others. Professor Bentley wonders if there may possibly be some unknown connection between the "(observing the Caution in the License)" in the Stationers' Register and the "(some-times)" on the title page, a connection conceivably involving a suppression of performances of the drama.[5]

There was no other printing of *Perkin Warbeck* in the seventeenth century. In 1714 a duodecimo edition was published with a thirteen-page history of the Warbeck episode immediately following the title page. On December 19, 1745, the play was acted at Goodman's Fields; very likely the abridged and revised manuscript copy of the play at the Bodleian Library was written for this performance.[6]

The present edition is based on a collation of six copies of the 1634 quarto (the only seventeenth-century edition): those at the British Museum (B.M.644.b.38), the Library of Congress, and Yale University as well as three at the Bodleian Library: Malone 158(4), Malone 238(5), and Art.G.33. Alterations were made in the text while the sheets were passing through the press. Corrections, in substantives and accidentals, have been found in the outer formes of sheets F and H and on the last leaf [L] among the copies collated. These, as concern substantive readings, are recorded in the textual notes.

DONALD K. ANDERSON, JR.

University of Missouri

[5] Bentley, III, 455–456.

[6] See Donald K. Anderson, Jr., "The Date and Handwriting of a Manuscript Copy of Ford's *Perkin Warbeck*," *Notes and Queries*, Vol. 10, No. 9 (Sept., 1963), 340–341.

PERKIN WARBECK

To the Rightly Honorable

William Cavendish,

Earl of Newcastle,

Viscount Mansfield,

Lord Bolsover and Ogle.   5

MY LORD:

Out of the darkness of a former age (enlighten'd by a late
both learned and an honorable pen), I have endeavored to
personate a great attempt, and in it a greater danger. In
other labors, you may read actions of antiquity discours'd;   10
in this abridgment, find the actors themselves discoursing, in
some kind practic'd as well what to speak as speaking why to
do. Your lordship is a most competent judge in expressions
of such credit, commissioned by your known ability in
examining, and enabled by your knowledge in determining,   15
the monuments of time. Eminent titles may indeed inform
who their owners are, not often what. To yours, the addition
of that information in both cannot in any application be
observ'd flattery, the authority being established by truth.
I can only acknowledge the errors in writing mine own, the   20
worthiness of the subject written being a perfection in the
story and of it. The custom of your lordship's entertainments
(even to strangers) is rather an example than a fashion: in
which consideration I dare not profess a curiosity, but am
only studious that your lordship will please, amongst such   25
as best honor your goodness, to admit into your noble
construction

John Ford.

---

2. *William Cavendish*] William Cavendish (1592–1676), Earl of Newcastle,
was a patron of many writers, among them Jonson, Shirley, and D'Avenant.
He was created Duke of Newcastle in 1665.

7–8. *late . . . pen*] very likely a reference to Bacon, whose *History of the
Reign of King Henry VII* (1622) was one of Ford's principal sources.

16. *monuments of time*] "such as are destined to live to future ages"
(Gifford).

To my own friend, Master John Ford, on his justifiable poem of Perkin Warbeck, this ode.

They who do know me know that I
    (Unskill'd to flatter)
  Dare speak this piece, in words, in matter,
A work, without the danger of the lie.
Believe me, friend, the name of this and thee   5
    Will live, your story.
  Books may want faith, or merit, glory;
This, neither, without judgment's lethargy.
When the arts dote, then some sick poet may
    Hope that his pen   10
  In new-stain'd paper can find men
To roar, "He is the wit's; his noise doth sway."
But such an age cannot be known; for all,
    Ere that time be,
  Must prove such truth, mortality.   15
So, friend, thy honor stands too fixt to fall.

                    GEORGE DONNE.

To his worthy friend, Master John Ford, upon his Perkin Warbeck.

Let men who are writ poets lay a claim
To the Phoebean hill; I have no name
Nor art in verse. True, I have heard some tell
Of Aganippe, but ne'er knew the well,
Therefore have no ambition with the times   5
To be in print for making of ill rimes.

[Commendatory poem by George Donne]
  7. *want*] lack.
  8. *without*] except in the case of.
  9. *dote*] act foolishly or stupidly.
  12. *noise . . . sway*] voice prevails.
  15. *prove*] experience.
  17. *George Donne*] possibly the son (b. 1605) of John Donne, the famous poet and clergyman. The son was captain and sergeant-major in the expedition at the Isle of Ré.
[Commendatory poem by Ralph Eure]
  2. *Phoebean hill*] Mount Olympus, home of Phoebus Apollo and the Muses.
  4. *Aganippe*] a fountain of Mount Helicon, sacred to the Muses.

But love of thee and justice to thy pen
Hath drawn me to this bar, with other men
To justify, though against double laws
(Waiving the subtle bus'ness of his cause),   10
The glorious Perkin, and thy poet's art,
Equal with his in playing the king's part.

RALPH EURE, *baronis primogenitus.*

To my faithful, no less deserving friend, the author, this indebted oblation.

Perkin is rediviv'd by thy strong hand
And crown'd a king of new. The vengeful wand
Of greatness is forgot: his execution
May rest unmention'd, and his birth's collusion
Lie buried in the story. But his fame   5
Thou hast eterniz'd, made a crown his game.
His lofty spirit soars yet. Had he been
Base in his enterprise, as was his sin
Conceiv'd, his title (doubtless) prov'd unjust,
Had, but for thee, been silenc'd in his dust.   10

GEORGE CRYMES, *miles.*

To the author, his friend, upon his Chronicle History.

These are not to express thy wit,
But to pronounce thy judgment fit
In full-fil'd phrase those times to raise
When Perkin ran his wily ways.
Still, let the method of thy brain   5
From error's touch and envy's stain

[Commendatory poem by Ralph Eure]
10. Waiving] Waving *Q*.

---

13. *Ralph Eure*] "the son of William, Lord Eure" (Ellis).
13. *baronis primogenitus*] first son of a baron.
[Commendatory poem by George Crymes]
1. *rediviv'd*] revived.
11. *miles*] soldier.

Preserve thee free, that e'er thy quill
Fair truth may wet, and fancy fill.
Thus graces are with muses met,
And practic critics on may fret.   10
For here thou hast produc'd a story
Which shall eclipse their future glory.

JOHN BROGRAVE, Ar.

To my friend and kinsman, Master John Ford, the author.

Dramatic poets (as the times go) now
Can hardly write what others will allow;
The cynic snarls, the critic howls and barks,
And ravens croak to drown the voice of larks.
Scorn those stage-harpies! This I'll boldly say: 5
Many may imitate, few match thy play.

JOHN FORD, Graiensis.

[Commendatory poem by John Brograve]
   10. *practic*] crafty, cunning.
[Commendatory poem by John Ford]
   7. *John Ford*] the playwright's cousin, to whom *Love's Sacrifice* was dedicated.
   7. *Graiensis*] of Gray's Inn. It was one of the four Inns of Court in London, legal societies that admitted persons to the practice of law.

PROLOGUE

Studies have of this nature been of late
So out of fashion, so unfollow'd, that
It is become more justice to revive
The antic follies of the times than strive
To countenance wise industry. No want   5
Of art doth render wit or lame or scant
Or slothful in the purchase of fresh bays,
But want of truth in them who give the praise
To their self-love, presuming to outdo
The writer or, for need, the actors too.   10
But such this author's silence best befits,
Who bids them be in love with their own wits.
From him to clearer judgments we can say
He shows a history couch'd in a play:
A history of noble mention, known,   15
Famous, and true; most noble, 'cause our own;
Not forg'd from Italy, from France, from Spain,
But chronicled at home; as rich in strain
Of brave attempts as ever fertile rage
In action could beget to grace the stage.   20
We cannot limit scenes, for the whole land
Itself appear'd too narrow to withstand
Competitors for kingdoms. Nor is here
Unnecessary mirth forc'd, to endear
A multitude. On these two rests the fate   25
Of worthy expectation: truth and state.

---

4. *antic*] grotesque, uncouthly ludicrous.
6. *or . . . or*] either . . . or.
7. *bays*] fame; in ancient times a garland of bay leaves was a token of
honor awarded to poets.
19. *rage*] strong emotion.

The Persons Presented

HENRY THE SEVENTH [, *King of England*]
[LORD] DAWBNEY
SIR WILLIAM STANLEY
[EARL OF] OXFORD } *[counselors to King Henry]*
[EARL OF] SURREY
[RICHARD FOX,] *Bishop of Durham*
URSWICK, *chaplain to King Henry*
SIR ROBERT CLIFFORD
LAMBERT SIMNEL
HIALAS, *a Spanish agent*
CONSTABLE, OFFICERS, SERVINGMEN, AND SOLDIERS

JAMES THE FOURTH, *King of Scotland*
EARL OF HUNTLEY } *[counselors to King James]*
EARL OF CRAWFORD
LORD DALIELL
MARCHMOUNT, *a herald*

PERKIN WARBECK
FRION, *his secretary*
[JOHN A WATER,] *Mayor of Cork*
HERON, *a mercer* } *[counselors to Warbeck]*
SKETON, *a tailor*
ASTLEY, *a scrivener*

LADY KATHERINE GORDON, *wife to Perkin*
COUNTESS OF CRAWFORD
JANE DOUGLAS, *Lady Katherine's maid*

[A POST, *serving King Henry*
A SERVANT, *attending Katherine*
EXECUTIONER, MASQUERS, HERALD, SHERIFF, ATTENDANTS]

The Scene, *The Continent of Great Britain*

The Chronicle History
of Perkin Warbeck

[I.i]

Enter King Henry; Durham; Oxford; Surrey; Sir William Stanley,
Lord Chamberlain; Lord Dawbney. *The* King *supported to his throne by*
Stanley *and* Durham. *A guard.*

KING HENRY.

Still to be haunted, still to be pursued,
Still to be frighted with false apparitions
Of pageant majesty and new-coin'd greatness,
As if we were a mockery king in state,
Only ordain'd to lavish sweat and blood   5
In scorn and laughter to the ghosts of York,
Is all below our merits; yet, my lords,
My friends and counselors, yet we sit fast
In our own royal birthright. The rent face
And bleeding wounds of England's slaughter'd people   10
Have been by us, as by the best physician,
At last both throughly cur'd and set in safety;
And yet for all this glorious work of peace
Ourself is scarce secure.
DURHAM.   The rage of malice
Conjures fresh spirits with the spells of York;   15
For ninety years ten English kings and princes,
Threescore great dukes and earls, a thousand lords
And valiant knights, two hundred fifty thousand
Of English subjects have in civil wars

---

12. *throughly*] thoroughly.
16–19. *For . . . wars*] contentions "which, for ninety Years, filled the
Wrinkles of the Face of our Commonwealth of England, with the Blood and
Sweat of ten Kings and Princes of the Race Royal: Sixty Dukes and Earls;
a thousand Lords and Knights, and an hundred and fifty thousand Soldiers
and People" (Gainsford, p. 164).

Been sacrific'd to an uncivil thirst   20
Of discord and ambition. This hot vengeance
Of the just powers above, to utter ruin
And desolation had reign'd on, but that
Mercy did gently sheathe the sword of justice
In lending to this blood-shrunk commonwealth   25
A new soul, new birth in your sacred person.

DAWBNEY.

Edward the Fourth, after a doubtful fortune,
Yielded to nature, leaving to his sons
Edward and Richard the inheritance
Of a most bloody purchase; these young princes   30
Richard the tyrant, their unnatural uncle,
Forc'd to a violent grave, so just is heaven.
Him hath your majesty by your own arm,
Divinely strengthen'd, pull'd from his boar's sty
And struck the black usurper to a carcass.   35
Nor doth the house of York decay in honors,
Though Lancaster doth repossess his right.
For Edward's daughter is King Henry's queen:
A blessed union, and a lasting blessing
For this poor panting island, if some shreds,   40
Some useless remnant of the house of York
Grudge not at this content.

OXFORD.   Margaret of Burgundy
Blows fresh coals of division.

SURREY.   Painted fires
Without or heat to scorch, or light to cherish.

DAWBNEY.

York's headless trunk her father, Edward's fate   45
Her brother king, the smothering of her nephews
By tyrant Gloucester brother to her nature,

44. or heat to] *1714;* to heate or *Q.*

---

23. *reign'd*] possibly wordplay. Weber, Gifford, and Coleridge print
reign'd; the 1714 edition, Dyce, and Ellis *rain'd* (Q "raign'd").
31. *Richard the tyrant*] Richard III.
34. *boar's*] "an allusion to the armorial bearings of Richard III"
(Coleridge).
42. *Margaret of Burgundy*] sister of Edward IV and widow of Duke
Charles the Bold.
47. *Gloucester*] Richard III.

Nor Gloucester's own confusion (all decrees
Sacred in heaven) can move this woman-monster,
But that she still from the unbottom'd mine   50
Of devilish policies doth vent the ore
Of troubles and sedition.

OXFORD.   In her age
(Great sir, observe the wonder) she grows fruitful,
Who in her strength of youth was always barren.
Nor are her births as other mothers' are,   55
At nine or ten months' end. She has been with child
Eight or seven years at least, whose twins being born
(A prodigy in nature) even the youngest
Is fifteen years of age at his first entrance
As soon as known i'th' world, tall striplings, strong   60
And able to give battle unto kings,
Idols of Yorkish malice.

DAWBNEY.   And but idols;
A steely hammer crushes 'em to pieces.

KING HENRY.

Lambert, the eldest, lords, is in our service,
Preferr'd by an officious care of duty   65
From the scullery to a falc'ner (strange example!),
Which shows the difference between noble natures
And the baseborn. But for the upstart duke,
The new reviv'd York, Edward's second son,
Murder'd long since i'th' Tower, he lives again   70
And vows to be your king.

STANLEY.   The throne is fill'd, sir.

KING HENRY.

True, Stanley, and the lawful heir sits on it;

62. S.P. DAWBNEY.] *Gifford; speech
assigned to Oxford in Q.*

---

57. *twins*] the impostors, Lambert Simnel and Perkin Warbeck.

60–61. *tall . . . kings*] "She bringeth forth tall striplings, able soon after
their coming into the world to bid battle to mighty Kings" (Bacon, XI,
220).

64. *Lambert*] Lambert Simnel claimed to be Edward, Earl of Warwick,
nephew of Edward IV. The real earl was alive in the Tower (where Henry
had imprisoned him), but rumors persisted that he had died there.

65. *officious*] eager to serve.

A guard of angels and the holy prayers
Of loyal subjects are a sure defense
Against all force and counsel of intrusion.   75
But now, my lords, put case some of our nobles,
Our great ones, should give countenance and courage
To trim Duke Perkin; you will all confess
Our bounties have unthriftily been scatter'd
Amongst unthankful men.
DAWBNEY.   Unthankful beasts,   80
Dogs, villains, traitors.
KING HENRY.   Dawbney, let the guilty
Keep silence. I accuse none, though I know
Foreign attempts against a state and kingdom
Are seldom without some great friends at home.
STANLEY.

Sir, if no other abler reasons else   85
Of duty or allegiance could divert
A headstrong resolution, yet the dangers
So lately passed by men of blood and fortunes
In Lambert Simnel's party must command
More than a fear, a terror to conspiracy.   90
The highborn Lincoln, son to De la Pole;
The Earl of Kildare; Lord Geraldine;
Francis, Lord Lovell; and the German baron,
Bold Martin Swart, with Broughton and the rest
(Most spectacles of ruin, some of mercy)   95
Are precedents sufficient to forewarn
The present times, or any that live in them,
What folly, nay, what madness 'twere to lift
A finger up in all defense but yours,
Which can be but imposturous in a title.   100
KING HENRY.

Stanley, we know thou lov'st us, and thy heart
Is figur'd on thy tongue; nor think we less
Of any's here. How closely we have hunted

---

76. *put case*] suppose.
91–94. *Lincoln . . . Broughton*] Supporters of Simnel, they led Yorkist
forces defeated by Henry's army near Stoke-on-Trent in 1487. Lincoln,
Geraldine, and Swart were slain; Lovell and Broughton disappeared; and
Kildare received clemency.

This cub, since he unlodg'd, from hole to hole,
Your knowledge is our chronicle: first Ireland,   105
The common stage of novelty, presented
This gewgaw to oppose us; there the Geraldines
And Butlers once again stood in support
Of this collossic statue. Charles of France
Thence call'd him into his protection,   110
Dissembled him the lawful heir of England,
Yet this was all but French dissimulation
Aiming at peace with us, which being granted
On honorable terms on our part, suddenly
This smoke of straw was pack'd from France again   115
T' infect some grosser air. And now we learn
(Maugre the malice of the bastard Nevill,
Sir Taylor, and a hundred English rebels)
They're all retir'd to Flanders, to the dam
That nurs'd this eager whelp, Margaret of Burgundy.   120
But we will hunt him there too; we will hunt him,
Hunt him to death even in the beldam's closet,
Though the archduke were his buckler.

SURREY.   She has styl'd him
"The fair white rose of England."

DAWBNEY.   Jolly gentleman,
More fit to be a swabber to the Flemish   125
After a drunken surfeit.

                    Enter Urswick.

URSWICK.   Gracious sovereign,
Please you peruse this paper.

DURHAM.   The king's countenance
Gathers a sprightly blood.

112–115. *Yet . . . again*] "But all this on the French King's part was but
a trick, the better to bow King Henry to peace. And therefore upon the
first grain of incense that was sacrificed upon the altar of peace at Bulloigne,
Perkin was smoked away" (Bacon, XI, 209).

117. *Maugre*] in spite of.

117–118. *Nevill . . . rebels*] They had joined Warbeck in Paris.

122. *beldam's*] old woman's.

123. *archduke*] Maximilian of Austria.

124. *fair . . . England*] The white rose was the emblem of the Yorkists;
the red rose, that of the Lancastrians.

125. *swabber*] "a sea-term for the boy who sweeps the decks" (Weber).

DAWBNEY.   Good news, believe it.
KING HENRY.
    Urswick, thine ear. —Th'ast lodg'd him?
URSWICK.   Strongly safe, sir.
KING HENRY.
    Enough. Is Barley come too?
URSWICK.   No, my lord.   130
KING HENRY.
    No matter; phew, he's but a running weed,
    At pleasure to be pluck'd up by the roots.
    But more of this anon. —I have bethought me.
    My lords, for reasons which you shall partake,
    It is our pleasure to remove our court   135
    From Westminster to th' Tower. We will lodge
    This very night there. Give, Lord Chamberlain,
    A present order for it.
STANLEY [aside].   The Tower!—I shall, sir.
KING HENRY.
    Come, my true, best, fast friends. These clouds will vanish;
    The sun will shine at full. The heavens are clearing.   140
                                        Exeunt. Flourish.

[I.ii]   Enter Huntley and Daliell.

HUNTLEY.
    You trifle time, sir.
DALIELL.   Oh my noble lord,
    You conster my griefs to so hard a sense
    That where the text is argument of pity,
    Matter of earnest love, your gloss corrupts it
    With too much ill-plac'd mirth.
HUNTLEY.   Much mirth, Lord Daliell?   5
    Not so, I vow. Observe me, sprightly gallant.
    I know thou art a noble lad, a handsome,
    Descended from an honorable ancestry,

---

129. *him*] Sir Robert Clifford. He and William Barley (l. 130) were
sent by Yorkists in England to visit Warbeck in Flanders. Clifford, having
been persuaded to shift his support to Henry, named to the king the
principal conspirators (see I.iii). Barley did not abandon Warbeck's cause
until later.
[I.ii]
    2. *conster*] construe.

Forward and active, dost resolve to wrestle
And ruffle in the world by noble actions   10
For a brave mention to posterity.
I scorn not thy affection to my daughter,
Not I, by good St. Andrew; but this bugbear,
This whoreson tale of honor (honor, Daliell)
So hourly chats and tattles in mine ear   15
The piece of royalty that is stitch'd up
In my Kate's blood, that 'tis as dangerous
For thee, young lord, to perch so near an eaglet
As foolish for my gravity to admit it.
I have spoke all at once.
DALIELL.   Sir, with this truth   20
You mix such wormwood that you leave no hope
For my disorder'd palate e'er to relish
A wholesome taste again; alas, I know sir,
What an unequal distance lies between
Great Huntley's daughter's birth and Daliell's fortunes.   25
She's the king's kinswoman, plac'd near the crown,
A princess of the blood, and I a subject.
HUNTLEY.
Right, but a noble subject. Put in that, too.
DALIELL.
I could add more, and in the rightest line
Derive my pedigree from Adam Mure,   30

---

13. *bugbear*] an object of needless dread.
14. *whoreson*] knavish.
   17. *Kate's blood*] Huntley had married the daughter of James I of Scotland.
   29–33. *I . . . day*] Elizabeth, daughter of Sir Adam Mure of Rowallan, was the first wife of Robert Fitz Alan, high steward, who became King Robert II; she was the mother of Robert III (born c. 1340) and the grandmother of James I of Scotland. The character of Daliell, it should be noted, is Ford's creation; no such person is mentioned by Bacon or Gainsford. But, as a matter of fact, the Daliell (or Dalzell) family was an ancient and honorable one: in 1296, Sir Thomas de Dalzell was one of the Scottish barons who swore fealty to Edward I, and it is possible that in that era the Daliell and Mure families did intermarry; in 1508 (nine years after War-beck's execution), Lord Robert Dalzell was killed at Dumfries in a skirmish between Lord Maxwell and Lord Crichton; in 1628 (when Ford was writing plays), Robert, Master of Dalzell, was created a lord; and, in 1639, his son Robert was made the first Earl of Carnwath. The hypothesis that Ford knew the contemporary Daliells and for that reason added "Lord Daliell" to his dramatis personae seems worth investigating.

A Scottish knight, whose daughter was the mother
To him who first begot the race of Jameses
That sway the scepter to this very day.
But kindreds are not ours when once the date
Of many years have swallowed up the memory   35
Of their originals. So pasture fields
Neighboring too near the ocean are supp'd up
And known no more. For stood I in my first
And native greatness, if my princely mistress
Vouchsaf'd me not her servant, 'twere as good   40
I were reduc'd to clownery, to nothing
As to a throne of wonder.

HUNTLEY [*aside*].   Now by Saint Andrew
A spark of mettle. 'A has a brave fire in him.
I would 'a had my daughter, so I knew 't not.
But must not be so, must not. —Well, young lord,   45
This will not do yet. If the girl be headstrong
And will not harken to good counsel, steal her
And run away with her; dance galliards, do,
And frisk about the world to learn the languages.
'Twill be a thriving trade; you may set up by 't.   50

DALIELL.

With pardon, noble Gordon, this disdain
Suits not your daughter's virtue, or my constancy.

HUNTLEY.

You are angry. —[*Aside*.] Would 'a would beat me, I
    deserve it.—
Daliell, thy hand; w'are friends. Follow thy courtship,
Take thine own time and speak. If thou prevail'st   55
With passion more than I can with my counsel,
She's thine, nay, she is thine, 'tis a fair match,
Free and allowed. I'll only use my tongue
Without a father's power; use thou thine.

37. supp'd] *Weber;* swoop'd *Gifford;*
soopd *Q.*

---

37. *supp'd*] swallowed up, consumed.
43. *spark*] a gallant young man.
43. *'A*] He.
48. *galliards*] lively French dances, for couples.

Self do, self have. No more words, win and wear her.   60
DALIELL.
  You bless me. I am now too poor in thanks
  To pay the debt I owe you.
HUNTLEY.   Nay, th'art poor
  Enough. —[*Aside*.]   I love his spirit infinitely.—
  Look ye, she comes. To her now, to her, to her.

Enter Katherine *and Jane*.

KATHERINE.
  The king commands your presence, sir.
HUNTLEY.   The gallant—   65
  This, this, this lord, this servant, Kate, of yours—
  Desires to be your master.
KATHERINE.   I acknowledge him
  A worthy friend of mine.
DALIELL.   Your humblest creature.
HUNTLEY [*aside*].
  So, so, the game's afoot. I'm in cold hunting;
  The hare and hounds are parties.
DALIELL.   Princely lady,   70
  How most unworthy I am to employ
  My services in honor of your virtues,
  How hopeless my desires are to enjoy
  Your fair opinion and, much more, your love
  Are only matter of despair, unless   75
  Your goodness give large warrant to my boldness,
  My feeble-wing'd ambition.
HUNTLEY [*aside*].   This is scurvy.
KATHERINE.
  My lord, I interrupt you not.
HUNTLEY [*aside*].   Indeed!
  Now, on my life, she'll court him. —Nay, nay, on, sir.
DALIELL.
  Oft have I tun'd the lesson of my sorrows   80
  To sweeten discord and enrich your pity;
  But all in vain. Here had my comforts sunk
  And never ris'n again to tell a story

---

60. *Self . . . have*] proverbial; cf. Tilley, S 217.

Of the despairing lover, had not now,
Even now, the earl your father—
HUNTLEY [*aside*]. 'A means me sure. 85
DALIELL.
After some fit disputes of your condition,
Your highness and my lowness, giv'n a license
Which did not more embolden than encourage
My faulting tongue.
HUNTLEY. How, how? How's that? Embolden?
Encourage? I encourage ye? D'ee hear, sir? 90
A subtle trick, a quaint one. Will you hear, man?
What did I say to you? Come, come, to th' point.
KATHERINE.
It shall not need, my lord.
HUNTLEY. Then hear me, Kate.—
Keep you on that hand of her, I on this.—
Thou stand'st between a father and a suitor, 95
Both striving for an interest in thy heart.
He courts thee for affection, I for duty;
He as a servant pleads, but by the privilege
Of nature though I might command, my care
Shall only counsel what it shall not force. 100
Thou canst but make one choice. The ties of marriage
Are tenures not at will, but during life.
Consider whose thou art, and who: a princess,
A princess of the royal blood of Scotland,
In the full spring of youth, and fresh in beauty. 105
The king that sits upon the throne is young
And yet unmarried, forward in attempts
On any least occasion to endanger
His person. Wherefore, Kate, as I am confident
Thou dar'st not wrong thy birth and education 110
By yielding to a common servile rage
Of female wantonness, so I am confident
Thou wilt proportion all thy thoughts to side
Thy equals, if not equal thy superiors.
My Lord of Daliell, young in years, is old 115

90. *D'ee*] Do ye.
113. *side*] match.

In honors, but nor eminent in titles
Or in estate that may support or add to
The expectation of thy fortunes. Settle
Thy will and reason by a strength of judgment.
For in a word, I give thee freedom, take it.   120
If equal fates have not ordain'd to pitch
Thy hopes above my height, let not thy passion
Lead thee to shrink mine honor in oblivion.
Thou art thine own; I have done.

DALIELL.   Oh y'are all oracle,
The living stock and root of truth and wisdom.   125

KATHERINE.
My worthiest lord and father, the indulgence
Of your sweet composition thus commands
The lowest of obedience. You have granted
A liberty so large that I want skill
To choose without direction of example: 130
From which I daily learn, by how much more
You take off from the roughness of a father,
By so much more I am engag'd to tender
The duty of a daughter. For respects
Of birth, degrees of title, and advancement,   135
I nor admire nor slight them; all my studies
Shall ever aim at this perfection only:
To live and die so, that you may not blush
In any course of mine to own me yours.

HUNTLEY.
Kate, Kate, thou grow'st upon my heart like peace,   140
Creating every other hour a jubilee.

KATHERINE.
To you, my Lord of Daliell, I address
Some few remaining words. The general fame
That speaks your merit, even in vulgar tongues,
Proclaims it clear; but in the best, a precedent.   145

HUNTLEY.
Good wench, good girl i' faith!

---

127. *composition*] mental constitution; "the combination of personal
qualities that make any one what he is" (*OED*).
141. *jubilee*] a period of rejoicing and festivity.

KATHERINE.   For my part, trust me,
    I value mine own worth at higher rate
    'Cause you are pleas'd to prize it. If the stream
    Of your protested service (as you term it)
    Run in a constancy more than a compliment,   150
    It shall be my delight that worthy love
    Leads you to worthy actions, and these guide ye
    Richly to wed an honorable name.
    So every virtuous praise in after ages
    Shall be your heir, and I in your brave mention   155
    Be chronicled the mother of that issue,
    That glorious issue.
HUNTLEY.   Oh that I were young again.
    She'd make me court proud danger, and suck spirit
    From reputation.
KATHERINE.   To the present motion,
    Here's all that I dare answer: when a ripeness   160
    Of more experience, and some use of time,
    Resolves to treat the freedom of my youth
    Upon exchange of troths, I shall desire
    No surer credit of a match with virtue
    Than such as lives in you. Meantime my hopes are   165
    Preserv'd secure, in having you a friend.
DALIELL.
    You are a blessed lady, and instruct
    Ambition not to soar a farther flight
    Than in the perfum'd air of your soft voice.—
    My noble Lord of Huntley, you have lent   170
    A full extent of bounty to this parley,
    And for it shall command your humblest servant.
HUNTLEY.
    Enough; we are still friends, and will continue
    A hearty love. —Oh Kate, thou art mine own!—
    No more. My Lord of Crawford.

Enter Crawford.

CRAWFORD.   From the king   175
    I come, my Lord of Huntley, who in council
    Requires your present aid.
HUNTLEY.   Some weighty business!

CRAWFORD.

A secretary from a Duke of York,
The second son to the late English Edward,
Conceal'd I know not where these fourteen years,   180
Craves audience from our master, and 'tis said
The duke himself is following to the court.

HUNTLEY.

Duke upon duke. 'Tis well, 'tis well; here's bustling
For majesty. My lord, I will along with ye.

CRAWFORD.

My service, noble lady.

KATHERINE.   Please ye walk, sir?   185

DALIELL [aside].

"Times have their changes; sorrow makes men wise.
The sun itself must set as well as rise."
Then why not I? —Fair madam, I wait on ye.   *Exeunt omnes.*

[I.iii]

    Enter Durham, Sir Robert Clifford, *and* Urswick. *Lights.*

DURHAM.

You find, Sir Robert Clifford, how securely
King Henry our great master doth commit
His person to your loyalty; you taste
His bounty and his mercy even in this,
That at a time of night so late, a place   5
So private as his closet, he is pleas'd
To admit you to his favor. Do not falter
In your discovery, but as you covet
A liberal grace and pardon for your follies,
So labor to deserve it by laying open   10
All plots, all persons that contrive against it.

URSWICK.

Remember not the witchcraft or the magic,
The charms and incantations which the sorceress

186–187.] Quotation marks were often used to indicate a sententious or
proverbial statement.
[I.iii]
  1. *securely*] confidently, without care or misgiving.
  6. *closet*] a king's private room for consultation or prayer.
  8. *discovery*] disclosure, revelation.

Of Burgundy hath cast upon your reason.
Sir Robert, be your own friend now, discharge   15
Your conscience freely. All of such as love you
Stand sureties for your honesty and truth.
Take heed you do not dally with the king;
He is wise as he is gentle.

CLIFFORD.   I am miserable
If Henry be not merciful.

URSWICK.   The king comes.   20

Enter King Henry.

KING HENRY.
Clifford!

CLIFFORD [*kneeling*].   Let my weak knees rot on the earth,
If I appear as leprous in my treacheries
Before your royal eyes, as to mine own
I seem a monster by my breach of truth.

KING HENRY.
Clifford, stand up. For instance of thy safety   25
I offer thee my hand.

CLIFFORD.   A sovereign balm
For my bruis'd soul, I kiss it with a greediness.
Sir, you are a just master, but I—

KING HENRY.   Tell me,
Is every circumstance thou hast set down
With thine own hand within this paper true?   30
Is it a sure intelligence of all
The progress of our enemies' intents
Without corruption?

CLIFFORD.   True, as I wish heaven,
Or my infected honor white again.

KING HENRY.
We know all, Clifford, fully, since this meteor,   35
This airy apparition first discradled

---

25. *instance*] proof.

35–40. *We . . . France*] "She [Margaret of Burgundy] began to cast with
herself from what coast this blazing star should first appear, and at what
time. It must be upon the horizon of Ireland; for there had the like meteor
strong influence before. The time of the apparition to be, when the King
should be engaged into a war with France" (Bacon, XI, 205).

36. *discradled*] left the cradle.

From Tournay into Portugal, and thence
Advanc'd his fiery blaze for adoration
To th' superstitious Irish; since the beard
Of this wild comet, conjur'd into France,   40
Sparkled in antic flames in Charles his court;
But shrunk again from thence and, hid in darkness,
Stole into Flanders, flourishing the rags
Of painted power on the shore of Kent,
Whence he was beaten back with shame and scorn,   45
Contempt, and slaughter of some naked outlaws.
But tell me, what new course now shapes Duke Perkin?

CLIFFORD.

For Ireland, mighty Henry; so instructed
By Stephen Frion, sometimes secretary
In the French tongue unto your sacred excellence,   50
But Perkin's tutor now.

KING HENRY.   A subtle villain,
That Frion. Frion—you, my Lord of Durham,
Knew well the man.

DURHAM.   French both in heart and actions.

KING HENRY.

Some Irish heads work in this mine of treason;
Speak 'em.

CLIFFORD.   Not any of the best; your fortune   55
Hath dull'd their spleens. Never had counterfeit
Such a confused rabble of lost bankrouts
For counselors: first Heron, a broken mercer;
Then John a Water, sometimes Mayor of Cork;
Sketon, a tailor; and a scrivener   60

---

37. *Tournay*] a city in Flanders.

56–61. *Never . . . Astley*] According to both Bacon and Gainsford, these
men became Warbeck's counselors after he had left Scotland. Ford, intro-
ducing them earlier in the story, portrays them as comical. Gainsford may
have suggested this viewpoint: "He had such poor Counsellors, as a Man
should smile at for Pity, rather than laugh at for Scorn . . . Understanding
Nothing but what consorted to their own Wilfulness, and outrageous
Appetites" (Gainsford, p. 202).

57. *bankrouts*] bankrupts.

58. *mercer*] a dealer in textile fabrics.

60. *scrivener*] a public clerk or scribe.

Call'd Astley. And whate'er these list to treat of,
Perkin must harken to. But Frion, cunning
Above these dull capacities, still prompts him
To fly to Scotland to young James the Fourth,
And sue for aid to him; this is the latest   65
Of all their resolutions.

KING HENRY.   Still more Frion.
Pestilent adder, he will hiss out poison
As dang'rous as infections; we must match 'em.
Clifford, thou hast spoke home, we give thee life.
But Clifford, there are people of our own   70
Remain behind untold. Who are they, Clifford?
Name those, and we are friends, and will to rest.
'Tis thy last task.

CLIFFORD.   Oh sir, here I must break
A most unlawful oath to keep a just one.

KING HENRY.
Well, well, be brief, be brief.

CLIFFORD.   The first in rank   75
Shall be John Ratcliffe, Lord Fitzwater, then
Sir Simon Mountford and Sir Thomas Thwaites,
With William Dawbney, Cressoner, Astwood,
Worsley the Dean of Paul's, two other friars,
And Robert Ratcliffe.

KING HENRY.   Churchmen are turn'd devils.   80
These are the principal?

CLIFFORD.   One more remains
Unnam'd, whom I could willingly forget.

KING HENRY.
Ha, Clifford, one more?

78. Cressoner] *Baskervill; Chessoner
Q.*

---

61. *list*] wish.

75–80. *first ... Ratcliffe*] Of these, according to Bacon, Fitzwater was
imprisoned in Calais, where, attempting to escape, he was beheaded.
"But Sir Symon Mountford, Robert Ratcliffe, and William Dawbeny,
were beheaded immediately after their condemnation. The rest were
pardoned, together with many others, clerks and laics, amongst which
were two Dominican friars, and William Worseley Dean of Paul's" (Bacon,
XI, 223).

CLIFFORD.   Great sir, do not hear him;
For when Sir William Stanley your lord chamberlain
Shall come into the list, as he is chief,   85
I shall lose credit with ye, yet this lord,
Last nam'd, is first against you.
KING HENRY.   Urswick, the light!—
View well my face, sirs; is there blood left in it?
DURHAM.
You alter strangely, sir.
KING HENRY.   Alter, Lord Bishop?
Why, Clifford stabb'd me, or I dream'd 'a stabb'd me.—   90
Sirrah, it is a custom with the guilty
To think they set their own stains off by laying
Aspersions on some nobler than themselves.
Lies wait on treasons, as I find it here.
Thy life again is forfeit. I recall   95
My word of mercy, for I know thou dar'st
Repeat the name no more.
CLIFFORD.   I dare, and once more
Upon my knowledge, name Sir William Stanley,
Both in his counsel and his purse, the chief
Assistant to the feign'd Duke of York.   100
DURHAM.
Most strange!
URSWICK.   Most wicked!
KING HENRY.   Yet again, once more.
CLIFFORD.
Sir William Stanley is your secret enemy,
And if time fit, will openly profess it.
KING HENRY.
Sir William Stanley! Who? Sir William Stanley
My chamberlain, my counselor, the love,   105
The pleasure of my court, my bosom friend,
The charge and the controlment of my person,

---

94. *Lies . . . treasons*] "Lies are ever attendants upon treason" (Weber).
104–108. *Sir . . . treasury*] "What, my Bosom Friend? My Counsellor?
My Chamberlain? . . . What, Sir William Stanley? He had the Government of my Chamber, and Charge and Comptrolment of all that are next
my person, the Love and Favour of our Court, and the very Keys of our
Treasury" (Gainsford, p. 185).
107. *controlment*] control.

The keys and secrets of my treasury,
The all of all I am. I am unhappy.
Misery of confidence—let me turn traitor   110
To mine own person, yield my scepter up
To Edward's sister and her bastard duke!

DURHAM.

You lose your constant temper.

KING HENRY.   Sir William Stanley!

Oh do not blame me; he, 'twas only he
Who, having rescu'd me in Bosworth Field   115
From Richard's bloody sword, snatch'd from his head
The kingly crown and plac'd it first on mine.
He never fail'd me; what have I deserv'd
To lose this good man's heart, or he his own?

URSWICK.

The night doth waste. This passion ill becomes ye;   120
Provide against your danger.

KING HENRY.   Let it be so.

Urswick, command straight Stanley to his chamber.
'Tis well we are i'th' Tower; set a guard on him.—
Clifford, to bed; you must lodge here tonight,
We'll talk with you tomorrow. —My sad soul   125
Divines strange troubles.

DAWBNEY [within].   Ho! The king, the king!

I must have entrance.

KING HENRY.   Dawbney's voice; admit him.

What new combustions huddle next to keep
Our eyes from rest?—

Enter Dawbney.

The news?

DAWBNEY.   Ten thousand Cornish,

Grudging to pay your subsidies, have gather'd   130
A head. Led by a blacksmith and a lawyer,
They make for London, and to them is join'd

129. S.D.] *Gifford; after* news *Q.*

---

130. *subsidies*] taxes.
131. *blacksmith . . . lawyer*] Michael Joseph and Thomas Flammock.

Lord Audley. As they march, their number daily
Increases; they are—
KING HENRY.   Rascals!—Talk no more;
Such are not worthy of my thoughts tonight.   135
And if I cannot sleep, I'll wake. —To bed.
When counsels fail and there's in man no trust,
Even then an arm from heaven fights for the just.   *Exeunt.*

[II.i]
Enter above, Countess of Crawford, Katherine, Jane, *with other ladies.*

COUNTESS OF CRAWFORD.

Come ladies, here's a solemn preparation
For entertainment of this English prince;
The king intends grace more than ordinary.
'Twere pity now, if 'a should prove a counterfeit.
KATHERINE.

Bless the young man, our nation would be laugh'd at   5
For honest souls through Christendom. My father
Hath a weak stomach to the business, madam,
But that the king must not be cross'd.
COUNTESS OF CRAWFORD.   'A brings
A goodly troop, they say, of gallants with him;
But very modest people, for they strive not   10
To fame their names too much; their godfathers
May be beholding to them, but their fathers
Scarce owe them thanks. They are disguised princes,
Brought up it seems to honest trades. No matter,
They will break forth in season.
JANE.   Or break out;   15
For most of 'em are broken, by report.—   *Flourish.*
The king.

138. S.D.] *Q adds: Finis Actus primi.*   16. S.D.] *Weber; after* silent (*l. 17*)
[II.i]   *Q.*

---

133. *Audley*] Lord Audley joined the Cornish at Wells, whence he led
them to Salisbury, Winchester, Kent, and Blackheath.
[II.i]
   6. *honest*] ingenuous.
  11. *fame*] to tell or spread abroad, report.
  15. *break forth*] proclaim (their names).
  15. *break out*] The probable meaning here is "escape from confinement,"
since *broken,* in the next line, very likely refers to their bankrupt state.

KATHERINE.   Let us observe 'em and be silent.

Enter King James, Huntley, Crawford, *and* Daliell [*with other noblemen*].

KING JAMES.

The right of kings, my lords, extends not only
To the safe conservation of their own,
But also to the aid of such allies   20
As change of time and state hath oftentimes
Hurl'd down from careful crowns to undergo
An exercise of sufferance in both fortunes.
So English Richard surnam'd Coeur-de-Lion,
So Robert Bruce our royal ancestor,   25
Forc'd by the trial of the wrongs they felt,
Both sought and found supplies from foreign kings
To repossess their own. Then grudge not, lords,
A much distressed prince. King Charles of France
And Maximilian of Bohemia both   30
Have ratified his credit by their letters.
Shall we then be distrustful? No, compassion
Is one rich jewel that shines in our crown,
And we will have it shine there.

HUNTLEY.   Do your will, sir.

KING JAMES.

The young duke is at hand. Daliell, from us   35
First greet him, and conduct him on; then Crawford
Shall meet him next, and Huntley last of all
Present him to our arms. Sound sprightly music,
Whilst majesty encounters majesty.   *Hautboys.*

Daliell *goes out, brings in* Perkin *at the door, where* Crawford *entertains
him, and from* Crawford, Huntley *salutes him and presents him to the*
King. *They embrace;* Perkin *in state retires some few paces back, during
which ceremony the noblemen slightly salute* Frion, Heron (*a mercer*),
Sketon (*a tailor*), Astley (*a scrivener*), *with* John a Water, *all Perkin's
followers. Salutations ended, cease music.*

39.5. Water] *Weber;* Watring *Q.*

22. *careful*] full of care.
24–28. *Richard . . . own*] Richard I had been aided by Philip II of France;
Robert I ("the Bruce"), by Edward I of England.

WARBECK.

    Most high, most mighty king! That now there stands   40
    Before your eyes, in presence of your peers,
    A subject of the rarest kind of pity
    That hath in any age touch'd noble hearts,
    The vulgar story of a prince's ruin
    Hath made it too apparent. Europe knows,   45
    And all the western world, what persecution
    Hath rag'd in malice against us, sole heir
    To the great throne of old Plantagenets.
    How from our nursery we have been hurried
    Unto the sanctuary, from the sanctuary   50
    Forc'd to the prison, from the prison hal'd
    By cruel hands to the tormentor's fury
    Is register'd already in the volume
    Of all men's tongues, whose true relation draws
    Compassion, melted into weeping eyes   55
    And bleeding souls. But our misfortunes since
    Have rang'd a larger progress through strange lands,
    Protected in our innocence by heaven.
    Edward the Fifth our brother, in his tragedy
    Quench'd their hot thirst of blood, whose hire to murder   60
    Paid them their wages of despair and horror;
    The softness of my childhood smil'd upon
    The roughness of their task and robb'd them farther
    Of hearts to dare or hands to execute.
    Great king, they spar'd my life, the butchers spar'd it,   65
    Return'd the tyrant, my unnatural uncle,
    A truth of my dispatch. I was convey'd
    With secrecy and speed to Tournay, foster'd

---

44. *vulgar*] widely disseminated.
49–52. *How . . . fury*] Warbeck describes himself as one "who hath been carried from the nursery to the sanctuary, from the sanctuary to the direful prison, from the prison to the hand of the cruel tormentor" (Bacon, XI, 245–246).
51. *hal'd*] dragged.
57. *progress*] a journey, often of an official nature.
60. *hire*] payment.
66. *unnatural*] inhuman.
67. *truth*] pledge.
67. *dispatch*] being put to death.

By obscure means, taught to unlearn myself.
But as I grew in years, I grew in sense   70
Of fear and of disdain: fear of the tyrant
Whose power sway'd the throne then, when disdain
Of living so unknown, in such a servile
And abject lowness, prompted me to thoughts
Of recollecting who I was. I shook off   75
My bondage and made haste to let my aunt
Of Burgundy acknowledge me her kinsman,
Heir to the crown of England, snatch'd by Henry
From Richard's head, a thing scarce known i'th' world.

KING JAMES.

My lord, it stands not with your counsel now   80
To fly upon invectives. If you can
Make this apparent what you have discours'd
In every circumstance, we will not study
An answer, but are ready in your cause.

WARBECK.

You are a wise and just king, by the powers   85
Above reserv'd beyond all other aids
To plant me in mine own inheritance:
To marry these two kingdoms in a love
Never to be divorc'd while time is time.
As for the manner, first of my escape,   90
Of my conveyance next, of my life since,
The means and persons who were instruments,
Great sir, 'tis fit I overpass in silence,
Reserving the relation to the secrecy
Of your own princely ear, since it concerns   95
Some great ones living yet, and others dead

89. divorc'd] *1714;* divor'd *Q.*

70–74. *But . . . lowness*] Warbeck says that he was "distracted between several passions, the one of fear to be known, lest the tyrant should have a new attempt upon me, the other of grief and disdain to be unknown and to live in that base and servile manner that I did" (Bacon, XI, 247).

80. *stands . . . counsel*] is not consistent with your purpose.

86. *reserv'd*] set apart for some fate or destiny.

90–97. *As . . . question'd*] "For the manner of my escape, it is fit it should pass in silence, or at least in a more secret relation; for that it may concern some alive, and the memory of some that are dead" (Bacon, XI, 247).

Whose issue might be question'd. For your bounty,
Royal magnificence to him that seeks it,
We vow hereafter to demean ourself
As if we were your own and natural brother,   100
Omitting no occasion in our person
To express a gratitude beyond example.

KING JAMES.

He must be more than subject, who can utter
The language of a king, and such is thine.
Take this for answer: be whate'er thou art,   105
Thou never shalt repent that thou hast put
Thy cause and person into my protection.
Cousin of York, thus once more we embrace thee.
Welcome to James of Scotland. For thy safety,
Know such as love thee not shall never wrong thee.   110
Come, we will taste a while our court delights,
Dream hence afflictions past, and then proceed
To high attempts of honor. On, lead on.
Both thou and thine are ours, and we will guard ye.
Lead on.   *Exeunt. Manent ladies above.*

COUNTESS OF CRAWFORD.   I have not seen a gentleman   115
Of a more brave aspect or goodlier carriage;
His fortunes move not him. —Madam, y'are passionate.

KATHERINE.

Beshrew me, but his words have touch'd me home,
As if his cause concern'd me; I should pity him
If 'a should prove another than he seems.   120

Enter Crawford.

CRAWFORD.

Ladies, the king commands your presence instantly
For entertainment of the duke.

---

97. *issue*] descendants.

98. *magnificence*] munificence.

105–107. *Take . . . protection*] "King James answered . . . That whosoever
he were, he should not repent him of putting himself into his hands"
(Bacon, XI, 249).

115. S.D. *Manent*] remain.

117. *passionate*] moved.

118. *Beshrew me*] a mild oath.

KATHERINE.   The duke
Must then be entertain'd, the king obey'd.
It is our duty.
COUNTESS OF CRAWFORD.   We will all wait on him.   *Exeunt.*

[II.ii]

     Flourish. Enter King Henry, Oxford, Durham, Surrey.

KING HENRY.
Have ye condemn'd my chamberlain?
DURHAM.   His treasons
Condemn'd him, sir, which were as clear and manifest
As foul and dangerous. Besides, the guilt
Of his conspiracy press'd him so nearly
That it drew from him free confession   5
Without an importunity.
KING HENRY.   Oh Lord Bishop,
This argued shame and sorrow for his folly,
And must not stand in evidence against
Our mercy and the softness of our nature;
The rigor and extremity of law   10
Is sometimes too, too bitter, but we carry
A chancery of pity in our bosom.
I hope we may reprieve him from the sentence
Of death; I hope we may.
DURHAM.   You may, you may;
And so persuade your subjects that the title   15
Of York is better, nay, more just and lawful
Than yours of Lancaster. So Stanley holds,
Which if it be not treason in the highest,
Then we are traitors all, perjur'd and false,
Who have took oath to Henry and the justice   20
Of Henry's title: Oxford, Surrey, Dawbney,
With all your other peers of state and church,
Forsworn, and Stanley true alone to heaven
And England's lawful heir.

---

4. *nearly*] closely.
12. *chancery*] "the highest court of judicature next to the House of
Lords"; one of its two tribunals "proceeded upon the rules of equity and
conscience, moderating the rigor of the common law" (*OED*).

OXFORD.   By Vere's old honors,
   I'll cut his throat dares speak it!
SURREY.   'Tis a quarrel   25
   To engage a soul in!
KING HENRY.   What a coil is here
   To keep my gratitude sincere and perfect.
   Stanley was once my friend, and came in time
   To save my life; yet to say truth, my lords,
   The man stay'd long enough t'endanger it.   30
   But I could see no more into his heart
   Than what his outward actions did present,
   And for 'em have rewarded 'em so fully
   As that there wanted nothing in our gift
   To gratify his merit, as I thought,   35
   Unless I should divide my crown with him
   And give him half; though now I well perceive
   'Twould scarce have serv'd his turn without the whole.
   But I am charitable, lords. Let justice
   Proceed in execution, whiles I mourn   40
   The loss of one whom I esteem'd a friend.
DURHAM.
   Sir, he is coming this way.
KING HENRY.   If 'a speak to me,
   I could deny him nothing; to prevent it,
   I must withdraw. Pray, lords, commend my favors
   To his last peace, which I with him will pray for.   45
   That done, it doth concern us to consult
   Of other following troubles.   *Exit.*
OXFORD.   I am glad
   He's gone. Upon my life he would have pardon'd
   The traitor, had 'a seen him.
SURREY.   'Tis a king
   Compos'd of gentleness—

47. S.D. *Exit.*] *Gifford; Exeunt Q.*

---

  24. *Vere's*] Oxford's family name.
  26. *coil*] turmoil.
  27. *sincere*] pure, unadulterated.
  28–30. *Stanley . . . it*] "The king's wit began now to suggest unto his passion, that Stanley at Bosworthfield, though he came time enough to save his life, yet he stayed long enough to endanger it" (Bacon, XI, 229–230).

DURHAM.   Rare and unheard of!   50
    But every man is nearest to himself,
    And that the king observes; 'tis fit 'a should.

       Enter Stanley, *Executioner,* Urswick, *and* Dawbney.

STANLEY.
    May I not speak with Clifford ere I shake
    This piece of frailty off?
DAWBNEY.   You shall, he's sent for.
STANLEY.
    I must not see the king?
DURHAM.   From him, Sir William,   55
    These lords and I am sent. He bade us say
    That he commends his mercy to your thoughts,
    Wishing the laws of England could remit
    The forfeit of your life as willingly
    As he would, in the sweetness of his nature,   60
    Forget your trespass; but howe'er your body
    Fall into dust, he vows, the king himself
    Doth vow, to keep a requiem for your soul,
    As for a friend close treasur'd in his bosom.
OXFORD.
    Without remembrance of your errors past,   65
    I come to take my leave, and wish you heaven.
SURREY.
    And I; good angels guard ye.
STANLEY.   Oh the king,
    Next to my soul, shall be the nearest subject
    Of my last prayers! My grave Lord of Durham,
    My Lords of Oxford, Surrey, Dawbney, all,   70
    Accept from a poor dying man a farewell.
    I was as you are once, great, and stood hopeful
    Of many flourishing years, but fate and time
    Have wheel'd about to turn me into nothing.

              Enter Clifford.

DAWBNEY.
    Sir Robert Clifford comes—the man, Sir William,   75
    You so desire to speak with.

---

51. *nearest*] most concerned for.

DURHAM.   Mark their meeting.

CLIFFORD.

Sir William Stanley, I am glad your conscience
Before your end hath emptied every burden
Which charg'd it, as that you can clearly witness
How far I have proceeded in a duty   80
That both concern'd my truth and the state's safety.

STANLEY.

Mercy, how dear is life to such as hug it!
Come hither. By this token think on me.
                    Makes a cross on Clifford's *face with his finger.*

CLIFFORD.

This token? What? I am abus'd!

STANLEY.   You are not.

I wet upon your cheeks a holy sign,   85
The cross, the Christian's badge, the traitor's infamy.
Wear, Clifford, to thy grave this painted emblem.
Water shall never wash it off; all eyes
That gaze upon thy face shall read there written
A state-informer's character, more ugly   90
Stamp'd on a noble name than on a base.
The heavens forgive thee!—Pray, my lords, no change
Of words; this man and I have us'd too many.

CLIFFORD.

Shall I be disgrac'd
Without reply?

DURHAM.   Give losers leave to talk; 95
His loss is irrecoverable.

STANLEY.   Once more

To all a long farewell. The best of greatness
Preserve the king. My next suit is, my lords,
To be remember'd to my noble brother,
Derby my much-griev'd brother. Oh persuade him   100
That I shall stand no blemish to his house
In chronicles writ in another age.
My heart doth bleed for him; and for his sighs,
Tell him he must not think the style of Derby,

---

92. *change*] exchange.   104. *style*] title.

Nor being husband to King Henry's mother, 105
The league with peers, the smiles of fortune, can
Secure his peace above the state of man.
I take my leave, to travel to my dust.
"Subjects deserve their deaths whose kings are just."—
[*To* Urswick.] Come, confessor. —[*To Executioner.*] On with
thy ax, friend, on. 110

Exeunt [Stanley, Urswick, *and Executioner*].

CLIFFORD.

Was I call'd hither by a traitor's breath
To be upbraided? Lords, the king shall know it.

Enter King Henry *with a white staff.*

KING HENRY.

The king doth know it, sir; the king hath heard
What he or you could say. We have given credit
To every point of Clifford's information, 115
The only evidence 'gainst Stanley's head.
'A dies for't, are you pleas'd?

CLIFFORD.   I pleas'd, my lord!

KING HENRY.

No echoes. For your service, we dismiss
Your more attendance on the court. Take ease
And live at home, but as you love your life, 120
Stir not from London without leave from us.
We'll think on your reward; away.

CLIFFORD.   I go, sir.   *Exit* Clifford.

KING HENRY.

Die all our griefs with Stanley. —Take this staff
Of office, Dawbney; henceforth be our chamberlain.

DAWBNEY.

I am your humblest servant.

KING HENRY.   We are followed 125
By enemies at home that will not cease
To seek their own confusion. 'Tis most true
The Cornish under Audley are march'd on
As far as Winchester. But let them come,

---

105. *Nor . . . mother*] Thomas Stanley, Earl of Derby, had married
Henry's mother before Henry became king.
129. *Winchester*] a city about sixty miles west of London.

Our forces are in readiness. We'll catch 'em   130
In their own toils.

DAWBNEY.   Your army, being muster'd,
Consist in all, of horse and foot, at least
In number six and twenty thousand—men
Daring and able, resolute to fight,
And loyal in their truths.

KING HENRY.   We know it, Dawbney.   135
For them, we order thus: Oxford in chief,
Assisted by bold Essex and the Earl
Of Suffolk, shall lead on the first battalia.—
[*To* Oxford.]   Be that your charge.

OXFORD.   I humbly thank your majesty.

KING HENRY.

The next division we assign to Dawbney.   140
These must be men of action, for on those
The fortune of our fortunes must rely.
The last and main, ourself commands in person,
As ready to restore the fight at all times
As to consummate an assured victory.   145

DAWBNEY.

The king is still oraculous.

KING HENRY.   But Surrey,
We have employment of more toil for thee.
For our intelligence comes swiftly to us
That James of Scotland late hath entertain'd
Perkin the counterfeit with more than common   150
Grace and respect, nay, courts him with rare favors.
The Scot is young and forward; we must look for
A sudden storm to England from the north,
Which to withstand, Durham shall post to Norham,

---

131. *toils*] traps.

136–145. *For . . . victory*] "He divided them into three parts. The first
was led by the Earl of Oxford in chief, assisted by the Earls of Essex and
Suffolk. . . . The second part of his forces (which were those that were to
be most in action, and upon which he relied most for the fortune of the
day) he did assign to be led by the Lord Chamberlain. . . . The third part
of his forces . . . he retained about himself, to be ready upon all events; to
restore the fight or consummate the victory" (Bacon, XI, 269–270).

138. *battalia*] "one of the large divisions of an army" (*OED*).

146. *oraculous*] oracular.

To fortify the castle and secure   155
The frontiers against an invasion there.
Surrey shall follow soon with such an army
As may relieve the bishop and encounter
On all occasions the death-daring Scots.
You know your charges all; 'tis now a time   160
To execute, not talk. Heaven is our guard still.
War must breed peace, such is the fate of kings.   *Exeunt.*

[II.iii]   *Enter* Crawford *and* Daliell.

CRAWFORD.
'Tis more than strange; my reason cannot answer
Such argument of fine imposture, couch'd
In witchcraft of persuasion, that it fashions
Impossibilities, as if appearance
Could cozen truth itself. This dukeling mushroom   5
Hath doubtless charm'd the king.
DALIELL.   'A courts the ladies
As if his strength of language chain'd attention
By power of prerogative.
CRAWFORD.   It madded
My very soul to hear our master's motion:
What surety both of amity and honor   10
Must of necessity ensue upon
A match betwixt some noble of our nation
And this brave prince, forsooth.
DALIELL.   'Twill prove too fatal;
Wise Huntley fears the threat'ning. Bless the lady
From such a ruin.
CRAWFORD.   How the council privy   15
Of this young Phaëthon do screw their faces
Into a gravity their trades, good people,
Were never guilty of! The meanest of 'em
Dreams of at least an office in the state.

---

155. *castle*] "Norham Castle. An ancient border castle on the S. bank of
the Tweed, 7 m. S.W. of Berwick" (Sugden).
[II.iii]
16. *Phaëthon*] son of Helios, the sun god, he tried to drive his father's sun
chariot and would have burned up the earth if Zeus had not destroyed
him with a thunderbolt.

DALIELL.

    Sure not the hangman's, 'tis bespoke already   20
    For service to their rogueships. —Silence!

Enter King James *and* Huntley.

KING JAMES.   Do not

    Argue against our will; we have descended
    Somewhat (as we may term it) too familiarly
    From justice of our birthright to examine
    The force of your allegiance—sir, we have—   25
    But find it short of duty.

HUNTLEY.   Break my heart,

    Do, do, king! Have my services, my loyalty
    (Heaven knows untainted ever) drawn upon me
    Contempt now in mine age, when I but wanted
    A minute of a peace not to be troubled,   30
    My last, my long one? Let me be a dotard,
    A bedlam, a poor sot, or what you please
    To have me, so you will not stain your blood
    (Your own blood, royal sir, though mix'd with mine),
    By marriage of this girl to a straggler!   35
    Take, take my head, sir! Whilst my tongue can wag,
    It cannot name him other.

KING JAMES.   Kings are counterfeits

    In your repute, grave oracle, not presently
    Set on their thrones, with scepters in their fists.
    But use your own detraction. 'Tis our pleasure   40
    To give our cousin York for wife our kinswoman,
    The Lady Katherine. Instinct of sovereignty
    Designs the honor, though her peevish father
    Usurps our resolution.

HUNTLEY.   Oh 'tis well,

    Exceeding well. I never was ambitious   45
    Of using conges to my daughter-queen.
    A queen? Perhaps a quean!—Forgive me, Daliell,

47. quean] *Weber; Queene Q.*

---

    32. *bedlam*] bedlamite, insane person.
    46. *conges*] polite bows made upon taking leave.
    47. *quean*] an ill-behaved woman; a strumpet.

Thou honorable gentleman. —None here
Dare speak one word of comfort?

DALIELL.   Cruel misery!

CRAWFORD.

The lady, gracious prince, may be hath settled   50
Affection on some former choice.

DALIELL.   Enforcement
Would prove but tyranny.

HUNTLEY.   I thank 'ee heartily.
Let any yeoman of our nation challenge
An interest in the girl, then the king
May add a jointure of ascent in titles,   55
Worthy a free consent; now 'a pulls down
What old desert hath builded.

KING JAMES.   Cease persuasions.
I violate no pawns of faiths, intrude not
On private loves. That I have play'd the orator
For kingly York to virtuous Kate, her grant   60
Can justify, referring her contents
To our provision. The Welsh Harry henceforth
Shall therefore know, and tremble to acknowledge,
That not the painted idol of his policy
Shall fright the lawful owner from a kingdom.   65
We are resolv'd.

HUNTLEY.   Some of thy subjects' hearts,
King James, will bleed for this!

KING JAMES.   Then shall their bloods
Be nobly spent. No more disputes; he is not
Our friend who contradicts us.

HUNTLEY.   Farewell, daughter!
My care by one is lessened. Thank the king for't,   70
I and my griefs will dance now. —Look, lords, look,
Here's hand in hand already!

KING JAMES.   Peace, old frenzy.—

70.] Q contains marginal S.D. "Enter."

53–54. *challenge . . . in*] assert a right in.
55. *jointure . . . titles*] "a dowry to bestow a title" (Struble).
61. *contents*] satisfaction, pleasure.
62. *provision*] providing.
62. *Welsh*] Owen Tudor, grandfather of Henry VII, was a Welshman.

Enter Warbeck, *leading* Katherine, *complimenting; Countess of Crawford,*
Jane, Frion, Mayor of Cork, Astley, Heron, *and* Sketon.

How like a king 'a looks! Lords, but observe
The confidence of his aspect. Dross cannot
Cleave to so pure a metal. Royal youth.   75
Plantagenet undoubted.

HUNTLEY [*aside*].   Ho, brave youth,
But no Plantagenet by'r Lady yet,
By red rose or by white.

WARBECK.   An union this way
Settles possession in a monarchy
Establish'd rightly, as is my inheritance.   80
Acknowledge me but sovereign of this kingdom,
Your heart, fair princess, and the hand of providence
Shall crown you queen of me and my best fortunes.

KATHERINE.
Where my obedience is, my lord, a duty,
Love owes true service.

WARBECK.   Shall I?—

KING JAMES.   Cousin, yes,   85
Enjoy her. From my hand accept your bride,
And may they live at enmity with comfort
Who grieve at such an equal pledge of troths.—
Y'are the prince's wife now.

KATHERINE.   By your gift, sir.

WARBECK.
Thus I take seizure of mine own.

KATHERINE.   I miss yet   90
A father's blessing. Let me find it. [*Kneels*.] Humbly
Upon my knees I seek it.

HUNTLEY.   I am Huntley,
Old Alexander Gordon, a plain subject,
Nor more, nor less; and lady, if you wish for
A blessing, you must bend your knees to heaven,   95
For heaven did give me you. Alas, alas,
What would you have me say? May all the happiness
My prayers ever sued to fall upon you

76. youth] *Weber;* Lady *Q.*

---

76. *brave*] handsome.

Preserve you in your virtues. —Prithee, Daliell,
Come with me, for I feel thy griefs as full   100
As mine; let's steal away and cry together.

DALIELL.

My hopes are in their ruins.   *Exeunt* Huntley *and* Daliell.

KING JAMES.   Good kind Huntley
Is overjoy'd. A fit solemnity
Shall perfit these delights. —Crawford, attend
Our order for the preparation.   105

Exeunt. Manent Frion, Mayor, Astley, Heron, *and* Sketon.

FRION.

Now worthy gentlemen, have I not followed
My undertakings with success? Here's entrance
Into a certainty above a hope.

HERON.

Hopes are but hopes. I was ever confident, when I traded
but in remnants, that my stars had reserv'd me to the title   110
of a viscount at least. Honor is honor though cut out of any
stuffs.

SKETON.

My brother Heron hath right wisely delivered his opinion,
for he that threads his needle with the sharp eyes of
industry shall in time go through-stitch, with the new suit   115
of preferment.

ASTLEY.

Spoken to the purpose, my fine-witted brother Sketon.
For as no indenture but has its counterpawn, no *noverint*
but his condition or defeasance; so no right but may have
claim, no claim but may have possession, any act of parlia-   120
ment to the contrary notwithstanding.

FRION.

You are all read in mysteries of state,
And quick of apprehension, deep in judgment,

---

104. *perfit*] perfect.

115. *go through-stitch*] complete thoroughly.

118. *counterpawn*] A counterpart, or counterpawn, was a copy (not the original) of an indenture.

118. *noverint*] a deed.

119. *defeasance*] a clause stating how the deed or contract might become void.

Active in resolution; and 'tis pity
Such counsel should lie buried in obscurity.   125
But why in such a time and cause of triumph,
Stands the judicious Mayor of Cork so silent?
Believe it sir, as English Richard prospers,
You must not miss employment of high nature.

MAYOR OF CORK.

If men may be credited in their mortality, which I dare 130
not peremptorily aver but they may or not be, presumptions
by this marriage are then, in sooth, of fruitful expectation.
Or else I must not justify other men's belief more than other
should rely on mine.

FRION.

Pith of experience! Those that have borne office   135
Weigh every word before it can drop from them.
But noble counselors, since now the present
Requires in point of honor (pray, mistake not)
Some service to our lord, 'tis fit the Scots
Should not engross all glory to themselves   140
At this so grand and eminent solemnity.

SKETON.

The Scots? The motion is defied. I had rather, for my
part, without trial of my country, suffer persecution under
the pressing iron of reproach or let my skin be punch'd full
of eyelet-holes with the bodkin of derision.   145

ASTLEY.

I will sooner lose both my ears on the pillory of forgery.

HERON.

Let me first live a bankrout and die in the lousy Hole of
hunger without compounding for sixpence in the pound.

MAYOR OF CORK.

If men fail not in their expectations, there may be spirits
also that digest no rude affronts, Master Secretary Frion, or 150
I am cozen'd—which is possible, I grant.

FRION.

Resolv'd like men of knowledge. At this feast, then,

144. punch'd] *Gifford;* pincht *Q.*

---

147. *Hole*] "one of the worst apartments of the Counter prison" (Dyce).
148. *compounding*] "of an insolvent person: To settle with creditors and
pay a fixed proportion in discharge of their full claims" (*OED*).

In honor of the bride, the Scots, I know,
Will in some show, some masque, or some device
Prefer their duties. Now it were uncomely   155
That we be found less forward for our prince
Than they are for their lady; and by how much
We outshine them in persons of account,
By so much more will our endeavors meet with
A livelier applause. Great emperors   160
Have for their recreations undertook
Such kind of pastimes. As for the conceit,
Refer it to my study; the performance
You all shall share a thanks in. 'Twill be grateful.

HERON.

The motion is allowed. I have stole to a dancing school when 165
I was a prentice.

ASTLEY.

There have been Irish hubbubs, when I have made one too.

SKETON.

For fashioning of shapes and cutting a cross-caper, turn me
off to my trade again.

MAYOR OF CORK.

Surely there is, if I be not deceived, a kind of gravity in   170
merriment; as there is, or perhaps ought to be, respect of
persons in the quality of carriage, which is, as it is con-
strued, either so, or so.

FRION.

Still you come home to me; upon occasion
I find you relish courtship with discretion,   175
And such are fit for statesmen of your merits.
Pray 'ee wait the prince, and in his ear acquaint him
With this design. I'll follow and direct 'ee.

                                    Exeunt. Manet Frion.

178.1.] *after* toil (*l. 179*) *Q*.

---

155. *Prefer*] proffer, present.
162. *conceit*] idea.
164. *grateful*] pleasurable.
167. *hubbubs*] "tumultuous merry-meetings at wakes and fairs" (Gifford).
168. *cross-caper*] a step in dancing.
174. *come home to*] "touch, affect, or move intimately" (*OED*).
175. *courtship*] conduct at court.

Oh the toil
Of humoring this abject scum of mankind,   180
Muddy-brain'd peasants! Princes feel a misery
Beyond impartial sufferance, whose extremes
Must yield to such abettors. Yet our tide
Runs smoothly without adverse winds. Run on!
Flow to a full sea! Time alone debates   185
Quarrels forewritten in the book of fates.   *Exit.*

[III.i]

Enter King Henry, *his gorget on, his sword, plume of feathers, leading
staff; and* Urswick.

KING HENRY.
How runs the time of day?
URSWICK.   Past ten, my lord.
KING HENRY.
A bloody hour will it prove to some,
Whose disobedience, like the sons o'th' earth,
Throw a defiance 'gainst the face of heaven.
Oxford, with Essex and stout De la Pole,   5
Have quieted the Londoners, I hope,
And set them safe from fear.
URSWICK.   They are all silent.
KING HENRY.
From their own battlements they may behold
Saint George's fields o'erspread with armed men,
Amongst whom our own royal standard threatens   10

---

185. *debates*] carries on.
[III.i]
   0.1. *gorget*] a piece of armor to protect the throat.
   0.1–0.2. *leading staff*] a baton or staff of a commanding officer.
   3. *sons o'th' earth*] the Titans, who rebelled unsuccessfully against the
gods of Olympus.
   5–7. *Oxford . . . fear*] "But the King . . . delivered them [the Londoners]
of this Fear: For he presently sent John Earl of Oxford, Henry Bourchier
Earl of Essex, Edmond de la Poole Earl of Suffolk . . . and other worthy
martial Men . . . to environ the Hill where the Rebels were incamped"
(Gainsford, pp. 197–198).
   9. *Saint George's fields*] "A large open space on the Surrey side of the
Thames between Southwark and Lambeth" (Sugden).

Confusion to opposers. We must learn
To practice war again in time of peace,
Or lay our crown before our subjects' feet.
Ha, Urswick, must we not?

URSWICK.   The powers who seated
King Henry on his lawful throne will ever   15
Rise up in his defense.

KING HENRY.   Rage shall not fright
The bosom of our confidence. In Kent
Our Cornish rebels, cozen'd of their hopes,
Met brave resistance by that country's earl,
George Abergeny, Cobham, Poynings, Guilford,   20
And other loyal hearts; now if Blackheath
Must be reserv'd the fatal tomb to swallow
Such stiff-neck'd abjects as with weary marches
Have travel'd from their homes, their wives, and children,
To pay instead of subsidies their lives,   25
We may continue sovereign. Yet Urswick,
We'll not abate one penny, what in parliament
Hath freely been contributed. We must not;
Money gives soul to action. Our competitor,
The Flemish counterfeit, with James of Scotland   30
Will prove what courage need and want can nourish
Without the food of fit supplies. But Urswick,
I have a charm in secret that shall loose
The witchcraft wherewith young King James is bound,
And free it at my pleasure without bloodshed.   35

URSWICK.
Your majesty's a wise king, sent from heaven
Protector of the just.

KING HENRY.   Let dinner cheerfully
Be serv'd in. This day of the week is ours,

---

20. *Abergeny* . . . *Guilford*] "But they [the rebels] were deceived in their
Expectation; For the Earl of Kent, George Lord Abergavenny, John
Brooke, Lord Cobham, Sir Edward Poinings, Sir Richard Guilford . . .
and many others . . . were . . . determined to offend them" (Gainsford,
p. 197).
21. *Blackheath*] "An extensive open common between Eltham and
Greenwich, 5 m. from the centre of London" (Sugden).
23. *abjects*] castaways, degraded persons.

Our day of providence; for Saturday
Yet never fail'd in all my undertakings   40
To yield me rest at night.   *A flourish.*
                    What means this warning?
Good fate, speak peace to Henry.

Enter Dawbney, Oxford, *and attendants.*

DAWBNEY.   Live the king,
Triumphant in the ruin of his enemies!
OXFORD.
The head of strong rebellion is cut off,
The body hew'd in pieces.
KING HENRY.
                    Dawbney, Oxford,   45
Minions to noblest fortunes, how yet stands
The comfort of your wishes?
DAWBNEY.   Briefly thus:
The Cornish under Audley disappointed
Of flattered expectation, from the Kentish
(Your majesty's right trusty liegemen) flew,   50
Feather'd by rage and hearten'd by presumption,
To take the field, even at your palace gates,
And face you in your chamber royal. Arrogance
Improv'd their ignorance, for they supposing
(Misled by rumor) that the day of battle   55
Should fall on Monday, rather brav'd your forces
Than doubted any onset; yet this morning,
When in the dawning I by your direction
Strove to get Deptford Strand Bridge, there I found

41. S.D.] *Weber; after* Henry (*l.42*)Q.   59. Deptford] *Weber; Dertford* Q.

39–41. *Saturday ... night*] After his victory at Bosworth Field, Henry "entered the City upon a Saturday, as he had also obtained the victory upon a Saturday; which day of the week, first upon observation, and after upon memory and fancy, he accounted and chose as a day prosperous unto him" (Bacon, XI, 52–53).

46. *Minions*] favorites.

51. *Feather'd*] winged, swift.

56. *brav'd*] treated with bravado.

57. *doubted*] suspected, anticipated.

59. *Deptford Strand Bridge*] according to Sugden, a bridge over the Ravensborne, where it flows into the Thames near London.

Such a resistance as might show what strength   60
Could make. Here arrows hail'd in showers upon us
A full yard long at least, but we prevail'd.
My Lord of Oxford with his fellow peers,
Environing the hill, fell fiercely on them
On the one side, I on the other, till, great sir   65
(Pardon the oversight), eager of doing
Some memorable act, I was engag'd
Almost a prisoner, but was freed as soon
As sensible of danger. Now the fight
Began in heat, which quenched in the blood   70
Of two thousand rebels, and as many more
Reserv'd to try your mercy, have return'd
A victory with safety.

KING HENRY.   Have we lost
An equal number with them?

OXFORD.   In the total
Scarcely four hundred. Audley, Flammock, Joseph,   75
The ringleaders of this commotion,
Railed in ropes, fit ornaments for traitors,
Wait your determinations.

KING HENRY.   We must pay
Our thanks where they are only due. Oh lords,
Here is no victory, nor shall our people   80
Conceive that we can triumph in their falls.
Alas, poor souls! Let such as are escap'd
Steal to the country back without pursuit.
There's not a drop of blood spilt but hath drawn
As much of mine; their swords could have wrought wonders   85
On their king's part, who faintly were unsheath'd
Against their prince, but wounded their own breasts.
Lords, we are debtors to your care.   Our payment
Shall be both sure and fitting your deserts.

DAWBNEY.

Sir, will you please to see those rebels, heads   90
Of this wild monster-multitude?

KING HENRY.   Dear friend,
My faithful Dawbney, no. On them our justice

---

77. *Railed*] tied in a row.

Must frown in terror; I will not vouchsafe
An eye of pity to them. Let false Audley
Be drawn upon an hurdle from the Newgate   95
To Tower Hill in his own coat of arms
Painted on paper, with the arms revers'd,
Defac'd, and torn; there let him lose his head.
The lawyer and the blacksmith shall be hang'd,
Quartered, their quarters into Cornwall sent,   100
Examples to the rest, whom we are pleas'd
To pardon and dismiss from further quest.—
My Lord of Oxford, see it done.

OXFORD.   I shall, sir.

KING HENRY.
Urswick.

URSWICK.   My lord?

KING HENRY.   To Dinham our high treasurer,
Say we command commissions be new granted   105
For the collection of our subsidies
Through all the west, and that speedily.—
Lords, we acknowledge our engagements due
For your most constant services.

DAWBNEY.   Your soldiers
Have manfully and faithfully acquitted   110
Their several duties.

KING HENRY.   For it, we will throw
A largess free amongst them, which shall hearten
And cherish up their loyalties. More yet
Remains of like employment; not a man
Can be dismiss'd till enemies abroad,   115
More dangerous than these at home, have felt
The puissance of our arms. Oh happy kings

---

95. *hurdle*] a frame or sled on which prisoners were drawn.
95. *Newgate*] Newgate prison.
96. *Tower Hill*] "The hill on the W. and N. of the T[ower] of Lond.
At the top of it, N.W. of the T[ower], a scaffold was kept in perpetuity for
the execution of state prisoners" (Sugden).
102. *quest*] "an official or judicial inquiry" (*OED*).
112. *largess*] "Handfuls of money cast among the people, or a donation
bestowed upon soldiers" (Weber).
113. *cherish up*] encourage.

Whose thrones are raised in their subjects' hearts!

Exeunt omnes.

[III.ii]   *Enter* Huntley *and* Daliell.

HUNTLEY.

Now sir, a modest word with you, sad gentleman.
Is not this fine, I trow, to see the gambols,
To hear the jigs, observe the frisks, b'enchanted
With the rare discord of bells, pipes, and tabors,
Hotchpotch of Scotch and Irish twingle-twangles,   5
Like to so many choristers of Bedlam
Trolling a catch? The feasts, the manly stomachs,
The healths in usquebaugh and bonnyclabber,
The ale in dishes never fetch'd from China,
The hundred thousand knacks not to be spoken of   10
(And all this for King Oberon and Queen Mab)
Should put a soul in t'ee. Look 'ee, good man,
How youthful I am grown. But by your leave,
This new queen-bride must henceforth be no more
My daughter; no, by'r Lady, 'tis unfit.   15
And yet you see how I do bear this change,
Methinks courageously; then shake off care
In such a time of jollity.

DALIELL.   Alas sir,
How can you cast a mist upon your griefs,
Which howsoe'er you shadow, but present   20
To any judging eye the perfect substance
Of which mine are but counterfeits?

HUNTLEY.   Foh Daliell,
Thou interrupts the part I bear in music
To this rare bridal feast. Let us be merry,
Whilst flattering calms secure us against storms.   25

15. My] *Q (corr.)*; Any *Q (uncorr.)*.

---

2. *gambols*] leaps or springs in dancing.
3. *frisks*] lively movements.
7. *Trolling a catch*] singing a round.
8. *usquebaugh*] whisky.
8. *bonnyclabber*] "curds-and-whey, or sour buttermilk" (Gifford).
10. *knacks*] tricks, devices.

Tempests when they begin to roar put out
The light of peace, and cloud the sun's bright eye
In darkness of despair; yet we are safe.

DALIELL.
    I wish you could as easily forget
    The justice of your sorrows, as my hopes   30
    Can yield to destiny.

HUNTLEY.   Pish, then I see
    Thou dost not know the flexible condition
    Of my apt nature. I can laugh, laugh heartily
    When the gout cramps my joints; let but the stone
    Stop in my bladder, I am straight a-singing;   35
    The quartan-fever shrinking every limb
    Sets me a-cap'ring straight. Do but betray me,
    And bind me a friend ever. What! I trust
    The losing of a daughter (though I doted
    On every hair that grew to trim her head)   40
    Admits not any pain like one of these.
    Come, th'art deceiv'd in me. Give me a blow,
    A sound blow on the face, I'll thank thee for't;
    I love my wrongs. Still th'art deceiv'd in me.

DALIELL.
    Deceiv'd? Oh noble Huntley, my few years   45
    Have learnt experience of too ripe an age
    To forfeit fit credulity. Forgive
    My rudeness, I am bold.

HUNTLEY.   Forgive me first
    A madness of ambition; by example
    Teach me humility, for patience scorns   50
    Lectures which schoolmen use to read to boys
    Uncapable of injuries. Though old
    I could grow tough in fury and disclaim
    Allegiance to my king, could fall at odds
    With all my fellow peers that durst not stand   55
    Defendants 'gainst the rape done on mine honor.

33. apt] Q (*corr.*); *not in* Q (*uncorr.*).   37. but] Q (*corr.*); *not in* Q (*uncorr.*).
35. Stop] Q (*corr.*); Stoppes Q
(*uncorr.*).

36. *quartan-fever*] "a fever characterized by the recurrence of a paroxysm
every fourth . . . day" (Struble).

But kings are earthly gods, there is no meddling
With their anointed bodies; for their actions,
They only are accountable to heaven.
Yet in the puzzle of my troubled brain   60
One antidote's reserv'd against the poison
Of my distractions; 'tis in thee t'apply it.

DALIELL.
Name it, oh name it quickly, sir!

HUNTLEY.   A pardon
For my most foolish slighting thy deserts.
I have cull'd out this time to beg it. Prithee   65
Be gentle; had I been so, thou hadst own'd
A happy bride, but now a castaway,
And never child of mine more.

DALIELL.   Say not so, sir;
It is not fault in her.

HUNTLEY.   The world would prate
How she was handsome; young I know she was,   70
Tender and sweet in her obedience;
But lost now. What a bankrupt am I made
Of a full stock of blessings. Must I hope
A mercy from thy heart?

DALIELL.   A love, a service,
A friendship to posterity.

HUNTLEY.   Good angels   75
Reward thy charity. I have no more
But prayers left me now.

DALIELL.   I'll lend you mirth, sir,
If you will be in consort.

HUNTLEY.   Thank ye truly.
I must, yes, yes, I must. Here's yet some ease,
A partner in affliction; look not angry.   80

DALIELL.
Good noble sir!   [*Flourish.*]

HUNTLEY.   Oh hark, we may be quiet,
The king and all the others come: a meeting
Of gaudy sights. This day's the last of revels;

---

75. *to posterity*] for posterity to remember.
78. *in consort*] accompanied.

Tomorrow sounds of war. Then new exchange:
Fiddles must turn to swords. —Unhappy marriage!   85

Flourish. Enter King James, Warbeck *leading* Katherine, Crawford,
Countess, and Jane. Huntley *and* Daliell *fall among them.*

KING JAMES.
    Cousin of York, you and your princely bride
    Have liberally enjoy'd such soft delights
    As a new-married couple could forethink,
    Nor has our bounty shorten'd expectation.
    But after all those pleasures of repose   90
    Or amorous safety, we must rouse the ease
    Of dalliance with achievements of more glory
    Than sloth and sleep can furnish. Yet, for farewell,
    Gladly we entertain a truce with time
    To grace the joint endeavors of our servants.   95
WARBECK.
    My royal cousin, in your princely favor
    The extent of bounty hath been so unlimited
    As only an acknowledgment in words
    Would breed suspicion in our state and quality.
    When we shall in the fullness of our fate   100
    (Whose minister, necessity, will perfit)
    Sit on our own throne, then our arms, laid open
    To gratitude in sacred memory
    Of these large benefits, shall twine them close
    Even to our thoughts and heart, without distinction.   105
    Then James and Richard, being in effect
    One person, shall unite and rule one people,
    Divisible in titles only.
KING JAMES.   Seat ye.
    Are the presenters ready?
CRAWFORD.   All are ent'ring.
HUNTLEY.
    Dainty sport toward, Daliell. Sit, come sit,   110
    Sit and be quiet. Here are kingly bug's-words.

---

101. *perfit*] cf. II.iii.104, note.
111. *bug's-words*] "swaggering or threatening language" (*OED*).

Enter at one door four Scotch antics, accordingly habited; enter at another four wild Irish in trouses, long-haired, and accordingly habited. Music. The masquers dance.

KING JAMES.
     To all a general thanks!

WARBECK.   In the next room
     Take your own shapes again; you shall receive
     Particular acknowledgment.   [*Exeunt masquers.*]

KING JAMES.   Enough
     Of merriments. —Crawford, how far's our army   115
     Upon the march?

CRAWFORD.   At Hedonhall, great king,
     Twelve thousand well prepar'd.

KING JAMES.   Crawford, tonight
     Post thither. We in person with the prince
     By four o'clock tomorrow after dinner
     Will be w'ee; speed away!

CRAWFORD.   I fly, my lord.   [*Exit.*] 120

KING JAMES.
     Our business grows to head now. —Where's your secretary
     That he attends 'ee not to serve?

WARBECK.   With Marchmount
     Your herald.

KING JAMES.   Good. The proclamation's ready;
     By that it will appear how the English stand
     Affected to your title. —Huntley, comfort   125
     Your daughter in her husband's absence; fight
     With prayers at home for us, who for your honors
     Must toil in fight abroad.

HUNTLEY.   Prayers are the weapons
     Which men so near their graves as I do use.
     I've little else to do.

KING JAMES.   To rest, young beauties!—   130

111.1. *antics*] clowns, burlesque performers.

111.2. *trouses*] close-fitting trousers with stockings attached, formerly worn by Irishmen and Scottish Highlanders.

120. *w'ee*] with ye.

123. *proclamation*] Ford makes no use of Warbeck's proclamation, a somewhat inaccurate version of which appears in Bacon (XI, 251–257). A transcript of the original is extant.

We must be early stirring, quickly part:
"A kingdom's rescue craves both speed and art."
Cousins, good night.   *Flourish.*

WARBECK.   Rest to our cousin king.

KATHERINE.

Your blessing, sir:

HUNTLEY.

Fair blessings on your highness; sure you need 'em.   135

> *Exeunt omnes; manent* Warbeck, [Jane,] *and* Katherine.

WARBECK.

Jane, set the lights down, and from us return
To those in the next room this little purse.
Say we'll deserve their loves.

JANE.   It shall be done, sir.   [*Exit.*]

WARBECK.

Now dearest, ere sweet sleep shall seal those eyes,
Love's precious tapers, give me leave to use   140
A parting ceremony; for tomorrow
It would be sacrilege to intrude upon
The temple of thy peace. Swift as the morning
Must I break from the down of thy embraces
To put on steel and trace the paths which lead   145
Through various hazards to a careful throne.

KATHERINE.

My lord, I would fain go w'ee; there's small fortune
In staying here behind.

WARBECK.   The churlish brow
Of war, fair dearest, is a sight of horror
For ladies' entertainment. If thou hear'st   150
A truth of my sad ending by the hand
Of some unnatural subject, thou withal
Shalt hear how I died worthy of my right
By falling like a king. And in the close
Which my last breath shall sound, thy name, thou fairest,   155
Shall sing a requiem to my soul, unwilling
Only of greater glory 'cause divided

---

154. *close*] "the conclusion of a musical phrase, theme or movement"
(*OED*).

From such a heaven on earth as life with thee.
But these are chimes for funerals; my business
Attends on fortune of a sprightlier triumph,   160
For love and majesty are reconcil'd,
And vow to crown thee empress of the west.

KATHERINE.
You have a noble language, sir; your right
In me is without question, and however
Events of time may shorten my deserts   165
In others' pity, yet it shall not stagger
Or constancy or duty in a wife.
You must be king of me, and my poor heart
Is all I can call mine.

WARBECK.   But we will live,
Live, beauteous virtue, by the lively test   170
Of our own blood, to let the counterfeit
Be known the world's contempt.

KATHERINE.   Pray do not use
That word, it carries fate in't. The first suit
I ever made, I trust your love will grant.

WARBECK.
Without denial, dearest.

KATHERINE.   That hereafter,   175
If you return with safety, no adventure
May sever us in tasting any fortune.
I ne'er can stay behind again.

WARBECK.   Y'are lady
Of your desires, and shall command your will;
Yet 'tis too hard a promise.

KATHERINE.   What our destinies   180
Have rul'd out in their books, we must not search,
But kneel to.   kniel to fate

WARBECK.   Then to fear when hope is fruitless
Were to be desperately miserable,
Which poverty our greatness dares not dream of,
And much more scorns to stoop to. Some few minutes   185
Remain yet; let's be thrifty in our hopes.   *Exeunt.*

---

181. *rul'd out*] decreed.
186. *thrifty*] thriving, successful.

[III.iii]   *Enter* King Henry, Hialas, *and* Urswick.

KING HENRY.
Your name is Pedro Hialas; a Spaniard?
HIALAS.
Sir, a Castilian born.
KING HENRY.   King Ferdinand
With wise Queen Isabel his royal consort,
Write 'ee a man of worthy trust and candor.
Princes are dear to heaven who meet with subjects   5
Sincere in their employments; such I find
Your commendation, sir. Let me deliver
How joyful I repute the amity
With your most fortunate master, who almost
Comes near a miracle in his success   10
Against the Moors, who had devour'd his country,
Entire now to his scepter. We for our part
Will imitate his providence, in hope
Of partage in the use on't. We repute
The privacy of his advisement to us   15
By you, intended an ambassador
To Scotland for a peace between our kingdoms:
A policy of love, which well becomes
His wisdom and our care.
HIALAS.   Your majesty
Doth understand him rightly.
KING HENRY.   Else,   20
Your knowledge can instruct me; wherein, sir,
To fall on ceremony would seem useless,
Which shall not need; for I will be as studious
Of your concealment in our conference
As any counsel shall advise.
HIALAS.   Then, sir,   25
My chief request is that, on notice given
At my dispatch in Scotland, you will send
Some learned man of power and experience
To join in treaty with me.

10–11. *success . . . Moors*] In 1492 the fall of Granada had marked the
end of Moorish power in Spain.
    13. *providence*] foresight.   14. *partage*] sharing.   14. *repute*] value.
    15. *advisement*] advice.   20. *Else*] if not.

KING HENRY.   I shall do it,
Being that way well provided by a servant   30
Which may attend 'ee ever.
HIALAS.   If King James
By any indirection should perceive
My coming near your court, I doubt the issue
Of my employment.
KING HENRY.   Be not your own herald;
I learn sometimes without a teacher.
HIALAS.   Good days   35
Guard all your princely thoughts.
KING HENRY.   Urswick, no further
Than the next open gallery attend him.—
A hearty love go with you.
HIALAS.   Your vow'd beadsman.
                    Exeunt Urswick *and* Hialas.
KING HENRY.
King Ferdinand is not so much a fox
But that a cunning huntsman may in time   40
Fall on the scent; in honorable actions
Safe imitation best deserves a praise.
                    Enter Urswick.
What, the Castilian's pass'd away?
URSWICK.   He is,
And undiscovered. The two hundred marks
Your majesty convey'd, 'a gently purs'd   45
With a right modest gravity.
KING HENRY.   What was't
'A mutter'd in the earnest of his wisdom?
'A spoke not to be heard. 'Twas about—
URSWICK.   Warbeck:
Now if King Henry were but sure of subjects,
Such a wild runagate might soon be cag'd,   50
No great ado withstanding.
KING HENRY.   Nay, nay, something
About my son Prince Arthur's match.

---

30. *servant*] i.e., Fox, Bishop of Durham.   33. *issue*] success.
38. *vow'd beadsman*] "vowed or devoted servant" (Gifford).
47. *earnest*] (1) ardour, zeal; (2) a foretaste or pledge of what is to come.
50. *runagate*] fugitive.

URSWICK.   Right, right, sir.
'A humm'd it out, how that King Ferdinand
Swore that the marriage 'twixt the Lady Katherine
His daughter, and the Prince of Wales your son,   55
Should never be consummated as long
As any Earl of Warwick liv'd in England,
Except by new creation.
KING HENRY.   I remember,
'Twas so indeed. The king his master swore it?
URSWICK.
Directly as he said.
KING HENRY.   An Earl of Warwick!—   60
Provide a messenger for letters instantly
To Bishop Fox. Our news from Scotland creeps,
It comes so slow. We must have airy spirits;
Our time requires dispatch. —The Earl of Warwick!
Let him be son to Clarence, younger brother   65
To Edward! Edward's daughter is I think
Mother to our Prince Arthur. —Get a messenger.   *Exeunt.*

[III.iv]
Enter King James, Warbeck, Crawford, Daliell, *Heron, Astley, Mayor,*
Sketon, and soldiers.

KING JAMES.
We trifle time against these castle walls;
The English prelate will not yield. Once more
Give him a summons.   *Parley.*

63. so] *Q* (*corr.*); too *Q* (*uncorr.*).

53–57. *Ferdinand . . . England*] Gainsford cites "a Speech of Ferdinando's
King of Spain, who should swear, that the Marriage between Lady
Catherine, his Daughter, and Prince Arthur of Wales, should never be
consummated, as long as any Earl of Warwick lived" (p. 210). As the male
heir of the house of York, Warwick threatened the Tudor succession.
Arthur and Katherine of Aragon were married in 1501.
    60. *Directly*] exactly.
[III.iv]
    3. S.D. *Parley*] "To beat or sound a parley, to call for or request a parley
[an informal conference with an enemy, under a truce] by sounding a
drum or trumpet" (*OED*).

Enter above, Durham, *armed, a truncheon in his hand, and soldiers.*

WARBECK.   See, the jolly clerk
Appears trimm'd like a ruffian!
KING JAMES.   Bishop, yet
Set ope the ports, and to your lawful sovereign,   5
Richard of York, surrender up this castle,
And he will take thee to his grace; else Tweed
Shall overflow his banks with English blood
And wash the sand that cements those hard stones
From their foundation.
DURHAM.   Warlike king of Scotland,   10
Vouchsafe a few words from a man enforc'd
To lay his book aside and clap on arms
Unsuitable to my age or my profession.
Courageous prince, consider on what grounds
You rend the face of peace and break a league   15
With a confederate king that courts your amity.
For whom too? For a vagabond, a straggler,
Not noted in the world by birth or name,
An obscure peasant, by the rage of hell
Loos'd from his chains to set great kings at strife.   20
What nobleman, what common man of note,
What ordinary subject hath come in,
Since first you footed on our territories,
To only feign a welcome? Children laugh at
Your proclamations, and the wiser pity   25
So great a potentate's abuse by one
Who juggles merely with the fawns and youth
Of an instructed compliment. Such spoils,
Such slaughters as the rapine of your soldiers
Already have committed, is enough   30
To show your zeal in a conceited justice.
Yet, great king, wake not yet my master's vengeance,

---

3. S.D. *truncheon*] a staff of office.
3. *clerk*] clergyman.   4. *trimm'd*] armed.
5. *ports*] portals, gates.
7. *Tweed*] "a river flowing into the North Sea at Berwick. During the latter part of its course it is the boundary between England and Scotland" (Sugden).
27. *fawns*] fawnings.   31. *conceited*] imagined.

But shake that viper off which gnaws your entrails.
I and my fellow subjects are resolv'd,
If you persist, to stand your utmost fury   35
Till our last blood drop from us.

WARBECK.   Oh sir, lend
No ear to this seducer of my honor!—
What shall I call thee, thou gray-bearded scandal,
That kick'st against the sovereignty to which
Thou owest allegiance?—Treason is bold-fac'd,   40
And eloquent in mischief. Sacred king,
Be deaf to his known malice!

DURHAM.   Rather yield
Unto those holy motions which inspire
The sacred heart of an anointed body.
It is the surest policy in princes   45
To govern well their own, than seek encroachment
Upon another's right.

CRAWFORD [aside].   The king is serious,
Deep in his meditations.

DALIELL [aside].   Lift them up
To heaven, his better genius!

WARBECK.   Can you study
While such a devil raves? Oh sir!

KING JAMES.   Well—bishop,   50
You'll not be drawn to mercy?

DURHAM.   Conster me
In like case by a subject of your own.
My resolution's fix'd. King James, be counsel'd:
A greater fate waits on thee.   *Exit* Durham *cum suis.*

KING JAMES.   Forage through
The country; spare no prey of life or goods.   55

WARBECK.
Oh sir, then give me leave to yield to nature;
I am most miserable. Had I been

37. No] *Weber;* Me *Q*.   48. meditations] *Gifford;* meditation
                                      Q.

---

51. *Conster*] construe.
54. S.D. *cum suis*] with his followers.
56. *yield to nature*] weep.

Born what this clergyman would by defame
Baffle belief with, I had never sought
The truth of mine inheritance with rapes   60
Of women or of infants murdered, virgins
Deflower'd, old men butchered, dwellings fir'd,
My land depopulated, and my people
Afflicted with a kingdom's devastation.
Show more remorse, great king, or I shall never   65
Endure to see such havoc with dry eyes.
Spare, spare my dear, dear England!

KING JAMES.   You fool your piety
Ridiculously, careful of an interest
Another man possesseth. Where's your faction?
Shrewdly the bishop guess'd of your adherents   70
When not a petty burgess of some town,
No, not a villager hath yet appear'd
In your assistance. That should make 'ee whine,
And not your country's sufferance, as you term it.

DALIELL [aside].
The king is angry.

CRAWFORD [aside].   And the passionate duke   75
Effeminately dolent.

WARBECK.   The experience
In former trials, sir, both of mine own
Or other princes cast out of their thrones,
Have so acquainted me how misery
Is destitute of friends, or of relief,   80
That I can easily submit to taste
Lowest reproof without contempt or words.

                    Enter Frion.

KING JAMES.
An humble-minded man!—Now, what intelligence
Speaks Master Secretary Frion?

---

58. *defame*] defamation.
59–64. *I . . . devastation*] "For now I see . . . Houses must be fired,
Countries depopulated, Women ravished, Virgins defloured, Infants slain,
the Aged murthered, the Goods rifled, and the Whole Kingdom subject to
Devastation" (Gainsford, pp. 193–194).
65. *remorse*] pity.   67. *fool*] make foolish.
74. *sufferance*] suffering.   76. *dolent*] doleful, sorrowful.

FRION.   Henry
    Of England hath in open field o'erthrown   85
    The armies who oppos'd him in the right
    Of this young prince.
KING JAMES.   His subsidies, you mean.
    More, if you have it.
FRION.   Howard Earl of Surrey,
    Back'd by twelve earls and barons of the north,
    An hundred knights and gentlemen of name,   90
    And twenty thousand soldiers, is at hand
    To raise your siege. Brooke, with a goodly navy,
    Is admiral at sea, and Dawbney follows
    With an unbroken army for a second.
WARBECK.
    'Tis false! They come to side with us.
KING JAMES.   Retreat!   95
    We shall not find them stones and walls to cope with.
    Yet, Duke of York (for such thou sayest thou art),
    I'll try thy fortune to the height: to Surrey,
    By Marchmount, I will send a brave defiance
    For single combat. Once a king will venter   100
    His person to an earl, with condition
    Of spilling lesser blood. Surrey is bold,
    And James resolv'd.
WARBECK.   Oh rather, gracious sir,
    Create me to this glory, since my cause
    Doth interest this fair quarrel; valued least,   105
    I am his equal.
KING JAMES.   I will be the man.—
    March softly off. "Where victory can reap
    A harvest crown'd with triumph, toil is cheap."   *Exeunt omnes.*

---

87. *subsidies*] taxes, against which the Cornish had rebelled in protest.

88–92. *Surrey . . . siege*] "With twelve Earls and Barons of the North
Country, one-hundred Knights and Gentlemen of Name, and twenty-
thousand Soldiers . . . he [Surrey] came to raise the Siege" (Gainsford,
p. 199).

94. *unbroken*] intact, whole.

100. *Once*] for once.

100. *venter*] venture.

104. *Create me to*] advance me to.

105. *Doth interest*] is involved in.

[IV.i]   *Enter* Surrey, Durham, *soldiers, with drums and colors.*

SURREY.

Are all our braving enemies shrunk back,
Hid in the fogs of their distempered climate,
Not daring to behold our colors wave
In spite of this infected air? Can they
Look on the strength of Cundrestine defac'd,   5
The glory of Hedonhall devasted, that
Of Edington cast down, the pile of Fulden
O'erthrown, and this the strongest of their forts,
Old Ayton Castle, yielded and demolished,
And yet not peep abroad? The Scots are bold,   10
Hardy in battle, but it seems the cause
They undertake, considered, appears
Unjointed in the frame on't.

DURHAM.   Noble Surrey,
Our royal master's wisdom is at all times
His fortune's harbinger, for when he draws   15
His sword to threaten war, his providence
Settles on peace, the crowning of an empire.   *Trumpet.*

SURREY.

Rank all in order. 'Tis a herald's sound,
Some message from King James. Keep a fix'd station.

Enter Marchmount *and another herald in their coats.*

MARCHMOUNT.

From Scotland's awful majesty we come   20
Unto the English general.

---

2. *distempered*] intemperate.

5–9. *Cundrestine . . . demolished*] "He [Surrey] entered Scotland, defaced
the Castle of Cundrestins, demolished the Tower of Hedonhall, under-
mined the Tower of Edington, overthrew the Pile of Fulden, and sent
Norroy . . . to . . . Haiton Castle, the strongest Fortification between
Berwick and Edinburgh, to deliver the same; . . . at last it was surrendered,
their Lives only saved; who were no sooner departed . . . but our General
quite overthrew and demolished the same" (Gainsford, p. 199). According
to Sugden, Hedonhall (Edin's or Etin's Hall), Edington, Fulden (Foulden),
and Ayton all were close to Berwick. Cundrestine (Cunzierton) was a hill
near Jedburgh.

6. *devasted*] devastated.

7. *pile*] "a lofty mass of buildings; a large building" (*OED*).

13. *frame*] "an established order, plan, scheme, system" (*OED*).

SURREY.   To me? Say on.
MARCHMOUNT.

    Thus then: the waste and prodigal
    Effusion of so much guiltless blood
    As in two potent armies of necessity
    Must glut the earth's dry womb, his sweet compassion   25
    Hath studied to prevent; for which to thee,
    Great Earl of Surrey, in a single fight
    He offers his own royal person, fairly
    Proposing these conditions only: that
    If victory conclude our master's right,   30
    The earl shall deliver from his ransom
    The town of Berwick to him, with the fishgarths.
    If Surrey shall prevail, the king will pay
    A thousand pounds down present for his freedom,
    And silence further arms. So speaks King James.   35
SURREY.

    So speaks King James. So like a king 'a speaks!
    Heralds, the English general returns
    A sensible devotion from his heart,
    His very soul, to this unfellowed grace.
    For let the king know, gentle heralds, truly   40
    How his descent from his great throne, to honor
    A stranger subject with so high a title
    As his compeer in arms, hath conquered more
    Than any sword could do; for which (my loyalty
    Respected) I will serve his virtues ever   45
    In all humility. But Berwick, say

    26–34. *for . . . freedom*] "The King of Scots . . . sent . . . to the Earl of Surrey . . . a . . . Challenge either to encounter him Army to Army, or Body to Body; conditionally, that, if the Victory fell to his Majesty, the Earl should deliver and surrender for his Ransom the Town of Berwick with the Fish-garths of the same; if the Earl again were Victor, the King would pay one-thousand Pounds Sterling for his Redemption" (Gainsford, p. 199).

    32. *fishgarths*] weirs or dams for keeping or taking fish.

    38. *sensible*] acutely felt.

    43. *compeer*] one of equal rank, peer.

    45. *Respected*] adhered to.

    46–55. *But . . . condition*] "Thirdly [said Surrey], for the Town of Berwick, it was none of his, but the King his Master's . . . [who] himself might well judge in the Affairs of Princes, what was to be done. . . . Only he

Is none of mine to part with. "In affairs
Of princes, subjects cannot traffic rights
Inherent to the crown." My life is mine,
That I dare freely hazard. And (with pardon   50
To some unbrib'd vainglory) if his majesty
Shall taste a change of fate, his liberty
Shall meet no articles. If I fall, falling
So bravely, I refer me to his pleasure
Without condition; and for this dear favor,   55
Say, if not countermanded, I will cease
Hostility, unless provok'd.

MARCHMOUNT.   This answer
We shall relate unpartially.

DURHAM.   With favor,
Pray have a little patience. —[*Aside to* Surrey.]   Sir, you find
By these gay flourishes how wearied travail   60
Inclines to willing rest. Here's but a prologue,
However confidently utter'd, meant
For some ensuing acts of peace. Consider
The time of year, unseasonableness of weather,
Charge, barrenness of profit; and occasion   65
Presents itself for honorable treaty,
Which we may make good use of. I will back
As sent from you, in point of noble gratitude
Unto King James with these his heralds. You
Shall shortly hear from me, my lord, for order   70
Of breathing or proceeding; and King Henry,
Doubt not, will thank the service.

SURREY [*aside to* Durham].   To your wisdom,
Lord Bishop, I refer it.

DURHAM [*aside to* Surrey].   Be it so, then.

SURREY.
Heralds, accept this chain and these few crowns.

---

desired Pardon for a little Vain-glory, that if he conquered the King, he
would release him freely; if the King vanquished him, he would yield him
his Life, or pay such a Tribute . . . befitting . . . an Earl" (Gainsford, p. 200).
    53. *meet no articles*] require no conditions.
    54. *bravely*] in a fine or superior way.
    71. *breathing*] resting or pausing.   74. *chain*] ornament.

MARCHMOUNT.
 Our duty, noble general.
DURHAM.   In part   75
 Of retribution for such princely love,
 My lord the general is pleas'd to show
 The king your master his sincerest zeal
 By further treaty, by no common man;
 I will myself return with you.
SURREY.   Y'oblige   80
 My faithfulest affections t'ee, Lord Bishop.
MARCHMOUNT.
 All happiness attend your lordship.
SURREY.   Come, friends
 And fellow soldiers. We, I doubt, shall meet
 No enemies but woods and hills to fight with.
 Then 'twere as good to feed and sleep at home.   85
 We may be free from danger, not secure.   *Exeunt omnes.*

[IV.ii]   *Enter* Warbeck *and* Frion.

WARBECK.
 Frion, oh, Frion, all my hopes of glory
 Are at a stand! The Scottish king grows dull,
 Frosty, and wayward since this Spanish agent
 Hath mix'd discourses with him. They are private,
 I am not call'd to council now. Confusion   5
 On all his crafty shrugs! I feel the fabric
 Of my designs are tottering.
FRION.   Henry's policies
 Stir with too many engines.
WARBECK.   Let his mines,
 Shap'd in the bowels of the earth, blow up
 Works rais'd for my defense, yet can they never   10
 Toss into air the freedom of my birth
 Or disavow my blood Plantagenet's.

---

 76. *retribution*] repayment.
[IV.ii]
 6. *fabric*] frame, structure.
 8. *engines*] plots, snares.

I am my father's son still. But, oh, Frion,
When I bring into count with my disasters
My wife's compartnership, my Kate's, my life's,   15
Then, then my frailty feels an earthquake. Mischief
Damn Henry's plots! I will be England's king,
Or let my aunt of Burgundy report
My fall in the attempt deserv'd our ancestors.

FRION.

You grow too wild in passion. If you will   20
Appear a prince indeed, confine your will
To moderation.

WARBECK.   What a saucy rudeness
Prompts this distrust? If, if I will appear?
Appear a prince? Death throttle such deceits
Even in their birth of utterance. Cursed cozenage   25
Of trust! Ye make me mad. 'Twere best, it seems,
That I should turn impostor to myself,
Be mine own counterfeit, belie the truth
Of my dear mother's womb, the sacred bed
Of a prince murdered, and a living baffled.   30

FRION.

Nay, if you have no ears to hear, I have
No breath to spend in vain.

WARBECK.   Sir, sir, take heed!
Gold and the promise of promotion rarely
Fail in temptation.

FRION.   Why to me this?

WARBECK.   Nothing.
Speak what you will; we are not sunk so low   35
But your advice may piece again the heart
Which many cares have broken. You were wont
In all extremities to talk of comfort.
Have ye none left now? I'll not interrupt ye.
Good, bear with my distractions. If King James   40
Deny us dwelling here, next whither must I?
I prithee be not angry.

FRION.   Sir, I told ye

---

19. *deserv'd*] was worthy of.
25. *cozenage*] deception.
30. *baffled*] disgraced.

Of letters come from Ireland, how the Cornish
Stomach their last defeat and humbly sue
That, with such forces as you could partake,   45
You would in person land in Cornwall, where
Thousands will entertain your title gladly.

WARBECK.

Let me embrace thee, hug thee! Th'ast reviv'd
My comforts. If my cousin king will fail,
Our cause will never.

Enter Mayor, Heron, Astley, Sketon.

Welcome, my tried friends.   50
You keep your brains awake in our defense.—
Frion, advise with them of these affairs,
In which be wondrous secret; I will listen
What else concerns us here. Be quick and wary. *Exit* Warbeck.

ASTLEY.

Ah sweet young prince!—Secretary, my fellow counselors   55
and I have consulted, and jump all in one opinion directly,
that if this Scotch garboils do not fadge to our minds, we will
pell-mell run amongst the Cornish choughs presently, and
in a trice.

SKETON.

'Tis but going to sea and leaping ashore, cut ten or twelve   60
thousand unnecessary throats, fire seven or eight towns,
take half a dozen cities, get into the market place, crown
him Richard the Fourth, and the business is finish'd.

50. S.D.] *Weber; after* friends *Q.*

---

45. *as . . . partake*] "this may probably mean, 'as you can get for partners
in your fortunes'" (Weber).

47. *entertain*] maintain.

56. *consulted . . . opinion*] probably a play on words: the noun *sault*,
meaning "jump" or "leap," was current in the early seventeenth century,
and, if preceded by *con*, conceivably could be taken to mean "jump together." Such pseudo-etymology would be appropriate to Astley, who
continually speaks the Latinate jargon of a scrivener.

57. *garboils*] commotions.

57. *fadge*] suit, agree.

58. *choughs*] (1) the red-legged crow, most abundant in Cornwall,
called "the Cornish chough"; (2) a rustic (*chuff*, sometimes spelled *chough*
when a play on words was intended).

MAYOR OF CORK.

> I grant ye, quoth I, so far forth as men may do, no more than
> men may do; for it is good to consider, when consideration   65
> may be to the purpose. Otherwise still you shall pardon
> me, "Little said is soon amended."

FRION.

> Then you conclude the Cornish action surest?

HERON.

> We do so, and doubt not but to thrive abundantly. Ho my
> masters, had we known of the commotion when we set sail   70
> out of Ireland, the land had been ours ere this time.

SKETON.

> Pish, pish, 'tis but forebearing being an earl or a duke a
> month or two longer. I say, and say it again, if the work go
> not on apace, let me never see new fashion more. I warrant
> ye, I warrant ye, we will have it so, and so it shall be.   75

ASTLEY.

> This is but a cold phlegmatic country, not stirring enough
> for men of spirit. Give me the heart of England for my
> money.

SKETON.

> A man may batten there in a week only with hot loaves
> and butter, and a lusty cup of muscadine and sugar at break-   80
> fast, though he make never a meal all the month after.

MAYOR OF CORK.

> Surely, when I bore office I found by experience that to be
> much troublesome was to be much wise and busy. I have
> observed how filching and bragging has been the best
> service in these last wars, and therefore conclude peremp-   85
> torily on the design in England. If things and things may fall
> out, as who can tell what or how—but the end will show it.

FRION.

> Resolv'd like men of judgment. Here to linger
> More time is but to lose it. Cheer the prince,
> And haste him on to this; on this depends   90
> Fame in success, or glory in our ends.   *Exeunt omnes.*

---

67. *Little . . . amended*] proverbial. Cf. Tilley, L. 358.

80. *muscadine*] "a kind of wine brought from Crete; so called because it
has a flavor of musk" (Weber).

[IV.iii]
    Enter King James; Durham *and* Hialas *on either side.*

HIALAS.

  France, Spain, and Germany combine a league
  Of amity with England; nothing wants
  For settling peace through Christendom but love
  Between the British monarchs, James and Henry.

DURHAM.

  The English merchants, sir, have been receiv'd   5
  With general procession into Antwerp;
  The emperor confirms the combination.

HIALAS.

  The King of Spain resolves a marriage
  For Katherine his daughter, with Prince Arthur.

DURHAM.

  France courts this holy contract.

HIALAS.   What can hinder   10
  A quietness in England—

DURHAM.   But your suffrage
  To such a silly creature, mighty sir,
  As is but in effect an apparition,
  A shadow, a mere trifle?

HIALAS.   To this union
  The good of both the church and commonwealth   15
  Invite 'ee.

DURHAM.   To this unity, a mystery
  Of providence points out a greater blessing
  For both these nations than our human reason

    1–10. *France . . . contract*] Durham and Hialas described to James a
"holy and general League, wherein both the Emperor, France, and Spain
desire a Combination of Amity with England; there only wanted himself
to make the Number complete. . . . The Merchants of England have been
received into Antwerp with general Prosession, the Emperor is pleased with
this Combination, the King of Spain pretendeth a Marriage . . . ; Therefore . . . be not an Enemy . . . of all Christendom" (Gainsford, p. 201).
    2. *wants*] lacks.
    12–14. *silly . . . shadow*] "The Commissioners answered . . . that they
intended not . . . the Destruction of so silly a Creature . . . but make him to
shew the Truth . . . that . . . King James, might not be colluded with
Shadows and Apparitions" (Gainsford, p. 201).

Can search into. King Henry hath a daughter,
The Princess Margaret; I need not urge   20
What honor, what felicity can follow
On such affinity 'twixt two Christian kings
Inleagu'd by ties of blood. But sure I am,
If you, sir, ratify the peace propos'd,
I dare both motion and effect this marriage   25
For weal of both the kingdoms.

KING JAMES.   Dar'st thou, Lord Bishop?

DURHAM.

Put it to trial, royal James, by sending
Some noble personage to the English court
By way of embassy.

HIALAS.   Part of the business
Shall suit my mediation.

KING JAMES.   Well; what heaven   30
Hath pointed out to be, must be; you two
Are ministers, I hope, of blessed fate.
But herein only I will stand acquitted:
No blood of innocents shall buy my peace.
For Warbeck, as you nick him, came to me   35
Commended by the states of Christendom,
A prince, though in distress. His fair demeanor,
Lovely behavior, unappalled spirit
Spoke him not base in blood, however clouded.
The brute beasts have both rocks and caves to fly to,   40
And men the altars of the church; to us

19–23. *King . . . blood*] As Ford's audience well knew, James's marriage
to Margaret was to have a very important consequence: the accession of
their great-grandson, James VI of Scotland, to the English throne as James
I in 1603.

25. *motion*] propose.

26. *weal*] well-being.

34–42. *No . . . refuge*] "But the King of Scots . . . would not buy his
Peace with the Blood of Innocents, especially a Man . . . shewing all the
Marks of a distressed . . . Prince . . . commended by the Emperor . . . and
himself of fair Demeanour, sweet Behaviour, and of a most royal and well
esteemed Spirit. . . . The King of Scots would not consent to deliver Perkin
upon any Condition; but, as he came to him for Refuge, he should depart
untouched, and not by his Occasion be in worse Case than the brute
Beasts" (Gainsford, p. 201).

35. *nick*] nickname.

He came for refuge. "Kings come near in nature
Unto the gods in being touch'd with pity."
Yet, noble friends, his mixture with our blood,
Even with our own, shall no way interrupt   45
A general peace; only I will dismiss him
From my protection, throughout my dominions
In safety, but not ever to return.

HIALAS.
    You are a just king.
DURHAM.   Wise, and herein happy.
KING JAMES.
    Nor will we dally in affairs of weight.   50
Huntley, Lord Bishop, shall with you to England,
Ambassador from us. We will throw down
Our weapons; peace on all sides now. Repair
Unto our council. We will soon be with you.

HIALAS.
    Delay shall question no dispatch.   Heaven crown it.   55
                    Exeunt Durham *and* Hialas.

KING JAMES.
    A league with Ferdinand? A marriage
With English Margaret? A free release
From restitution for the late affronts?
Cessation from hostility? And all
For Warbeck not delivered, but dismiss'd?   60
We could not wish it better. —Daliell!

              Enter Daliell.

DALIELL.   Here, sir.
KING JAMES.
    Are Huntley and his daughter sent for?
DALIELL.   Sent for,
And come, my lord.
KING JAMES.   Say to the English prince,
We want his company.
DALIELL.   He is at hand, sir.

Enter Warbeck, Katherine, Jane, Frion, Heron, Sketon, Mayor,
Astley.

61. S.D.] *Weber; after* sir *Q.*

KING JAMES.

    Cousin, our bounty, favors, gentleness,   65
Our benefits, the hazard of our person,
Our people's lives, our land hath evidenc'd
How much we have engag'd on your behalf.
How trivial and how dangerous our hopes
Appear, how fruitless our attempts in war,   70
How windy, rather smoky, your assurance
Of party shows, we might in vain repeat.
But now obedience to the mother church,
A father's care upon his country's weal,
The dignity of state directs our wisdom   75
To seal an oath of peace through Christendom,
To which we are sworn already. 'Tis you
Must only seek new fortunes in the world
And find an harbor elsewhere. As I promis'd
On your arrival, you have met no usage   80
Deserves repentance in your being here,
But yet I must live master of mine own.
However, what is necessary for you
At your departure, I am well content
You be accommodated with, provided   85
Delay prove not my enemy.

WARBECK.   It shall not,
Most glorious prince. The fame of my designs
Soars higher than report of ease and sloth
Can aim at. I acknowledge all your favors
Boundless and singular, am only wretched   90
In words as well as means to thank the grace

65–77. *Cousin . . . already*] "King James began to expostulate and reason the Matter with him: First, From a Repetition of the Benefits and Favours received by his Princely Liberality and Gentleness. Secondly, From his Consanguinity, in marrying his Kinswoman upon dangerous Hopes and trivial Adventures. Thirdly, From his many Trials and sundry Conflicts in England, proving all his Promises Wind and Smoke. . . . Fourthly, Upon the new Combination of Amity with all the Princes of Europe. . . . Fifthly, Upon the fatherly Regard of his Country. . . . Last of all, from the Care of Religion and Mother-Church. . . . For . . . he was now interested in the Confederacy of the Peace of Christendom" (Gainsford, p. 201).

71. *windy*] unsubstantial.

71. *smoky*] evanescent (?).

That flow'd so liberally. Two empires firmly
You're lord of: Scotland, and Duke Richard's heart.   *loyalty*
My claim to mine inheritance shall sooner
Fail than my life to serve you, best of kings.   95
And witness Edward's blood in me, I am
More loath to part with such a great example
Of virtue than all other mere respects.
But sir, my last suit is you will not force
From me what you have given—this chaste lady,   100
Resolv'd on all extremes.

KATHERINE.   I am your wife;
No human power can or shall divorce
My faith from duty.   *duty or love?*

WARBECK.   Such another treasure
The earth is bankrout of.

KING JAMES.   I gave her, cousin,
And must avow the gift; will add withal   105
A furniture becoming her high birth
And unsuspected constancy; provide
For your attendance. We will part good friends.

                                   Exeunt King *and* Daliell.

WARBECK.
The Tudor hath been cunning in his plots;
His Fox of Durham would not fail at last.   110
But what? Our cause and courage are our own.
Be men, my friends, and let our cousin king
See how we follow fate as willingly
As malice follows us. Y'are all resolv'd
For the west parts of England?

OMNES.   Cornwall, Cornwall!   115

FRION.
The inhabitants expect you daily.

WARBECK.   Cheerfully
Draw all our ships out of the harbor, friends.

108.1. *Exeunt.*] *Exit. Q.*   115. S.P. OMNES.] *Q (corr.); not in Q
                                       (uncorr.).*

---

101. *Resolv'd . . . extremes*] resolute in all extremities.
106. *A furniture*] accessories.
107. *unsuspected*] not subject to suspicion.

Our time of stay doth seem too long. We must
Prevent intelligence; about it suddenly.

OMNES.

A prince, a prince, a prince!   *Exeunt* Counselors. 120

WARBECK.

Dearest, admit not into thy pure thoughts
The least of scruples, which may charge their softness
With burden of distrust. Should I prove wanting
To noblest courage now, here were the trial.
But I am perfect, sweet; I fear no change,   125
More than thy being partner in my sufferance.

KATHERINE.

My fortunes, sir, have arm'd me to encounter
What chance soe'er they meet with. —Jane, 'tis fit
Thou stay behind, for whither wilt thou wander?

JANE.

Never till death will I forsake my mistress,   130
Nor then, in wishing to die with 'ee gladly.

KATHERINE.

Alas good soul.

FRION.   Sir, to your aunt of Burgundy
I will relate your present undertakings;
From her expect on all occasions, welcome.
You cannot find me idle in your services.   135

WARBECK.

Go, Frion, go! Wise men know how to soothe
Adversity, not serve it; thou hast waited
Too long on expectation. "Never yet
Was any nation read of so besotted
In reason, as to adore the setting sun."   140
Fly to the archduke's court; say to the duchess,
Her nephew, with fair Katherine his wife,
Are on their expectation to begin
The raising of an empire. If they fail,

120. S.P. OMNES.] *Q (corr.)*; *not in Q*
(*uncorr.*).

---

119. *Prevent intelligence*] act before our movements are made known.
125. *perfect*] completely assured.

Yet the report will never. Farewell, Frion.   *Exit* Frion. 145
This man, Kate, has been true, though now of late
I fear too much familiar with the Fox.

Enter Huntley *and* Daliell.

HUNTLEY.

I come to take my leave. You need not doubt
My interest in this sometime child of mine.
She's all yours now, good sir. —Oh poor lost creature,   150
Heaven guard thee with much patience. If thou canst
Forget thy title to old Huntley's family,
As much of peace will settle in thy mind
As thou canst wish to taste but in thy grave.
Accept my tears yet, prithee; they are tokens   155
Of charity as true as of affection.

KATHERINE.

This is the cruel'st farewell!

HUNTLEY.   Love, young gentleman,
This model of my griefs. She calls you husband.
Then be not jealous of a parting kiss;
It is a father's not a lover's off'ring.   160
Take it, my last. —I am too much a child.
Exchange of passion is to little use;
So I should grow too foolish. Goodness guide thee!

Exit Huntley.

KATHERINE.

Most miserable daughter!—Have you aught
To add, sir, to our sorrows?

DALIELL.   I resolve,   165
Fair lady, with your leave, to wait on all
Your fortunes in my person, if your lord
Vouchsafe me entertainment.

WARBECK.

We will be bosom friends, most noble Daliell,
For I accept this tender of your love   170
Beyond ability of thanks to speak it.—
Clear thy drown'd eyes, my fairest; time and industry
Will show us better days, or end the worst.   *Exeunt omnes.*

163. *So*] thus.

[IV.iv]   *Enter* Oxford *and* Dawbney.

OXFORD.

No news from Scotland yet, my lord?

DAWBNEY.   Not any
But what King Henry knows himself. I thought
Our armies should have march'd that way; his mind,
It seems, is altered.

OXFORD.   Victory attends
His standard everywhere.

DAWBNEY.   Wise princes, Oxford,   5
Fight not alone with forces. Providence
Directs and tutors strength; else elephants
And barbed horses might as well prevail
As the most subtle stratagems of war.

OXFORD.

The Scottish king show'd more than common bravery   10
In proffer of a combat hand to hand
With Surrey.

DAWBNEY.   And but show'd it. Northern bloods
Are gallant being fir'd, but the cold climate,
Without good store of fuel, quickly freezeth
The glowing flames.

OXFORD.   Surrey, upon my life,   15
Would not have shrunk an hair's breadth.

DAWBNEY.   May 'a forfeit
The honor of an English name, and nature,
Who would not have embrac'd it with a greediness
As violent as hunger runs to food.
'Twas an addition any worthy spirit   20
Would covet next to immortality,
Above all joys of life. We all miss'd shares
In that great opportunity.

                    Enter King Henry *and* Urswick, *whispering.*

OXFORD.   The king!
See, 'a comes smiling.

---

6. *Providence*] foresight.
8. *barbed*] "armed . . . with a barb or bard . . . a protective covering for
the breast and flanks of a war-horse" (*OED*).
20. *addition*] honor.

DAWBNEY.   Oh the game runs smooth
On his side, then, believe it. Cards well shuffled   25
And dealt with cunning bring some gamester thrift,
But others must rise losers.

KING HENRY.   The train takes?

URSWICK.
Most prosperously.

KING HENRY.   I knew it should not miss.
He fondly angles who will hurl his bait
Into the water 'cause the fish at first   30
Plays round about the line and dares not bite.—
Lords, we may reign your king yet. Dawbney, Oxford,
Urswick, must Perkin wear the crown?

DAWBNEY.   A slave!

OXFORD.
A vagabond!

URSWICK.   A glowworm!

KING HENRY.   Now if Frion,
His practic'd politician, wear a brain   35
Of proof, King Perkin will in progress ride
Through all his large dominions. Let us meet him,
And tender homage. Ha, sirs? Liegemen ought
To pay their fealty.

DAWBNEY.   Would the rascal were
With all his rabble within twenty miles   40
Of London.

KING HENRY.   Farther off is near enough
To lodge him in his home. I'll wager odds
Surrey and all his men are either idle
Or hasting back; they have not work, I doubt,
To keep them busy.

DAWBNEY.   'Tis a strange conceit, sir.   45

KING HENRY.
Such voluntary favors as our people
In duty aid us with, we never scatter'd
On cobweb parasites, or lavish'd out

---

26. *thrift*] prosperity, success.
27. *train*] trick, snare.
29. *fondly*] foolishly.
44. *doubt*] fear.

In riot or a needless hospitality.
No undeserving favorite doth boast   50
His issues from our treasury; our charge
Flows through all Europe, proving us but steward
Of every contribution, which provides
Against the creeping canker of disturbance.
Is it not rare then, in this toil of state   55
Wherein we are embark'd with breach of sleep,
Cares, and the noise of trouble, that our mercy
Returns nor thanks nor comfort? Still the west
Murmur and threaten innovation,
Whisper our government tyrannical,   60
Deny us what is ours, nay, spurn their lives,
Of which they are but owners by our gift.
It must not be.

OXFORD.   It must not, should not.

Enter a Post.

KING HENRY.   So then.—
To whom?

POST.   This packet to your sacred majesty.

KING HENRY.
Sirrah, attend without.   [*Exit* Post.] 65

OXFORD.
News from the north, upon my life.

DAWBNEY.   Wise Henry
Divines aforehand of events; with him
Attempts and execution are one act.

KING HENRY [*aside to* Urswick].
Urswick, thine ear. Frion is caught, the man
Of cunning is outreach'd. We must be safe.   70
Should reverend Morton our archbishop move
To a translation higher yet, I tell thee

63. S.D.] *Weber; after* whom (*l. 64*)
Q.

---

51. *issues*] money.
59. *innovation*] revolution.
71. *Morton*] John Morton, Archbishop of Canterbury.
71–72. *move . . . yet*] i.e., die.

My Durham owns a brain deserves that see.
He's nimble in his industry, and mounting.
Thou hear'st me?
URSWICK.   And conceive your highness fitly.   75
KING HENRY.
Dawbney and Oxford, since our army stands
Entire, it were a weakness to admit
The rust of laziness to eat amongst them.
Set forward toward Salisbury; the plains
Are most commodious for their exercise.   80
Ourself will take a muster of them there,
And or disband them with reward, or else
Dispose as best concerns us.
DAWBNEY.   Salisbury?
Sir, all is peace at Salisbury.
KING HENRY.   Dear friend,
The charge must be our own; we would a little   85
Partake the pleasure with our subjects' ease.
Shall I entreat your loves?
OXFORD.   Command our lives.
KING HENRY.
Y'are men know how to do, not to forethink.
My bishop is a jewel tried and perfect;
A jewel, lords. The post who brought these letters   90
Must speed another to the Mayor of Exeter.—
Urswick, dismiss him not.
URSWICK.   He waits your pleasure.
KING HENRY.
Perkin a king? A king?
URSWICK.   My gracious lord.
KING HENRY.
Thoughts busied in the sphere of royalty
Fix not on creeping worms without their stings,   95
Mere excrements of earth. The use of time

---

73. *see*] the center of authority or jurisdiction of a bishop, in this instance
Canterbury. Actually, Fox in 1501 was made bishop of Winchester, considered the richest bishopric in England.

74. *mounting*] ambitious.

79. *Salisbury*] a city about eighty miles southwest of London. It is midway
between London and Exeter, which Warbeck was to attack.

Is thriving safety, and a wise prevention
Of ills expected. W'are resolv'd for Salisbury.   *Exeunt omnes.*

[IV.v]
A general shout within. Enter Warbeck, Daliell, Katherine, *and* Jane.

WARBECK.

After so many storms as wind and seas
Have threaten'd to our weather-beaten ships,
At last, sweet fairest, we are safe arriv'd
On our dear mother earth, ingrateful only
To heaven and us in yielding sustenance   5
To sly usurpers of our throne and right.
These general acclamations are an omen
Of happy process to their welcome lord.
They flock in troops, and from all parts with wings
Of duty fly to lay their hearts before us.   10
Unequal'd pattern of a matchless wife,
How fares my dearest yet?

KATHERINE.   Confirm'd in health,
By which I may the better undergo
The roughest face of change; but I shall learn
Patience to hope, since silence courts affliction,   15
For comforts to this truly noble gentleman—
Rare, unexampled pattern of a friend—
And my beloved Jane, the willing follower
Of all misfortunes.

DALIELL.   Lady, I return
But barren crops of early protestations,   20
Frost-bitten in the spring of fruitless hopes.

JANE.

I wait but as the shadow to the body,
For madam, without you let me be nothing.

WARBECK.

None talk of sadness; we are on the way
Which leads to victory. Keep cowards thoughts   25
With desperate sullenness! The lion faints not
Lock'd in a grate, but loose, disdains all force

---

8. *process*] progress, advance.
27. *grate*] cage.

Which bars his prey; and we are lion-hearted,
Or else no king of beasts.   *Another shout* [*within*].
                Hark how they shout,
Triumphant in our cause! Bold confidence   30
Marches on bravely, cannot quake at danger.

                Enter Sketon.

SKETON.

Save King Richard the Fourth, save thee, king of hearts!
The Cornish blades are men of mettall, have proclaimed
through Bodmin and the whole county my sweet prince
monarch of England. Four thousand tall yeomen with bow   35
and sword already vow to live and die at the foot of King
Richard.

                Enter Astley.

ASTLEY.

The mayor our fellow counselor is servant for an emperor.
Exeter is appointed for the rendezvous, and nothing wants
to victory but courage and resolution. *Sigillatum et datum*   40
decimo Septembris, anno regni regis primo, et caetera; confirmatum
est. All's cocksure.

WARBECK.

To Exeter, to Exeter, march on!
Commend us to our people. We in person
Will lend them double spirits. Tell them so.   45

SKETON AND ASTLEY.

King Richard, King Richard!

WARBECK.

A thousand blessings guard our lawful arms!
A thousand horrors pierce our enemies' souls!

29. S.D.] *Gifford; after* shout Q.   34. Bodmin] *Dyce; Bodnam* Q.

---

33. *blades . . . mettall*] possible wordplay on *metal* and *mettle*. Bacon
writes: ". . . the Cornishmen were become like metal often fired and
quenched, churlish, and that would sooner break than bow; swearing and
vowing not to leave him till the uttermost drop of their blood were spilt"
(XI, 288).

34. *Bodmin*] a town in Cornwall, about twenty-five miles northwest of
Plymouth.

40–42. *Sigillatum . . . est*] "Sealed and dated on the tenth of September,
in the first year of the king's [Warbeck's] reign, etc.; confirmed."

Pale fear unedge their weapons' sharpest points,
And when they draw their arrows to the head,   50
Numbness shall strike their sinews. Such advantage
Hath majesty in its pursuit of justice
That on the proppers-up of truth's old throne
It both enlightens counsel and gives heart
To execution, whiles the throats of traitors   55
Lie bare before our mercy. Oh divinity
Of royal birth! How it strikes dumb the tongues
Whose prodigality of breath is brib'd
By trains to greatness! Princes are but men,
Distinguish'd in the fineness of their frailty,   60
Yet not so gross in beauty of the mind,
For there's a fire more sacred purifies
The dross of mixture. Herein stands the odds:
"Subjects are men; on earth, kings men and gods."

Exeunt omnes.

[V.i]

Enter Katherine *and* Jane *in riding suits, with one* Servant.

KATHERINE.

It is decreed; and we must yield to fate,
Whose angry justice, though it threaten ruin,
Contempt, and poverty, is all but trial
Of a weak woman's constancy in suffering.
Here in a stranger's and an enemy's land,   5
Forsaken and unfurnish'd of all hopes
But such as wait on misery, I range
To meet affliction wheresoe'er I tread.
My train and pomp of servants is reduc'd
To one kind gentlewoman and this groom.   10
Sweet Jane, now whither must we?
JANE.   To your ships,
Dear lady, and turn home.
KATHERINE.   Home! I have none.
Fly thou to Scotland, thou hast friends will weep
For joy to bid thee welcome. But oh, Jane,

---

63. *stands . . . odds*] lies the difference.

My Jane, my friends are desperate of comfort   15
As I must be of them; the common charity,
Good people's alms, and prayers of the gentle
Is the revenue must support my state.
As for my native country, since it once
Saw me a princess in the height of greatness   20
My birth allow'd me, here I make a vow
Scotland shall never see me, being fallen
Or lessened in my fortunes. Never, Jane,
Never to Scotland more will I return.
Could I be England's queen (a glory, Jane,   25
I never fawn'd on), yet the king who gave me
Hath sent me with my husband from his presence,
Deliver'd us suspected to his nation,
Render'd us spectacles to time and pity.
And is it fit I should return to such   30
As only listen after our descent
From happiness enjoy'd to misery
Expected, though uncertain? Never, never!
Alas, why dost thou weep, and that poor creature
Wipe his wet cheeks too? Let me feel alone   35
Extremities, who know to give them harbor.
Nor thou nor he has cause. You may live safely.

JANE.
There is no safety whiles your dangers, madam,
Are every way apparent.

SERVANT.   Pardon, lady,
I cannot choose but show my honest heart;   40
You were ever my good lady.

KATHERINE.   Oh dear souls,
Your shares in grief are too, too much!

Enter Daliell.

DALIELL.   I bring,
Fair princess, news of further sadness yet
Than your sweet youth hath been acquainted with.

KATHERINE.
Not more, my lord, than I can welcome; speak it.   45
The worst, the worst I look for.

---

15. *desperate*] without hope.

DALIELL.   All the Cornish
          At Exeter were by the citizens
          Repuls'd, encounter'd by the Earl of Devonshire
          And other worthy gentlemen of the country.
          Your husband march'd to Taunton and was there   50
          Affronted by King Henry's chamberlain,
          The king himself in person with his army
          Advancing nearer to renew the fight
          On all occasions. But the night before
          The battles were to join, your husband privately,   55
          Accompanied with some few horse, departed
          From out the camp and posted none knows whither.
KATHERINE.
          Fled without battle given?
DALIELL.   Fled, but follow'd
          By Dawbney; all his parties left to taste
          King Henry's mercy, for to that they yielded,   60
          Victorious without bloodshed.
KATHERINE.   Oh, my sorrows!
          If both our lives had prov'd the sacrifice
          To Henry's tyranny, we had fallen like princes
          And robb'd him of the glory of his pride.
DALIELL.
          Impute it not to faintness or to weakness   65
          Of noble courage, lady, but foresight;
          For by some secret friend he had intelligence
          Of being bought and sold by his base followers.
          Worse yet remains untold.
KATHERINE.   No, no, it cannot.
DALIELL.
          I fear y'are betray'd. The Earl of Oxford   70
          Runs hot in your pursuit.
KATHERINE.   'A shall not need.
          We'll run as hot in resolution gladly
          To make the earl our jailer.

---

          50. *Taunton*] a town about thirty miles northeast of Exeter.
          51. *Affronted*] confronted.
          51. *chamberlain*] i.e., Dawbney.
          55. *battles*] armies.
          59. *parties*] allies, partisans.

JANE.   Madam, madam,
    They come, they come!

                Enter Oxford, *with followers.*

DALIELL.   Keep back! Or he who dares
    Rudely to violate the law of honor   75
    Runs on my sword.
KATHERINE.   Most noble sir, forbear.—
    What reason draws you hither, gentlemen?
    Whom seek 'ee?
OXFORD.   All stand off!—With favor, lady,
    From Henry, England's king, I would present
    Unto the beauteous princess, Katherine Gordon,   80
    The tender of a gracious entertainment.
KATHERINE.
    We are that princess, whom your master king
    Pursues with reaching arms to draw into
    His power. Let him use his tyranny;
    We shall not be his subjects.
OXFORD.   My commission   85
    Extends no further, excellentest lady,
    Than to a service; 'tis King Henry's pleasure
    That you, and all that have relation t'ee,
    Be guarded as becomes your birth and greatness.
    For rest assur'd, sweet princess, that not aught   90
    Of what you do call yours shall find disturbance,
    Or any welcome other than what suits
    Your high condition.
KATHERINE.   By what title, sir,
    May I acknowledge you?
OXFORD.   Your servant, lady,
    Descended from the line of Oxford's earls,   95
    Inherits what his ancestors before him
    Were owners of.
KATHERINE.   Your king is herein royal,
    That by a peer so ancient in desert
    As well as blood commands us to his presence.
OXFORD.
    Invites 'ee, princess, not commands.

_____

93. *condition*] rank.

KATHERINE.   Pray use   100
    Your own phrase as you list; to your protection
    Both I and mine submit.
OXFORD.   There's in your number
    A nobleman whom fame hath bravely spoken.
    To him the king my master bade me say
    How willingly he courts his friendship: far   105
    From an enforcement, more than what in terms
    Of courtesy so great a prince may hope for.
DALIELL.
    My name is Daliell.
OXFORD.   'Tis a name hath won
    Both thanks and wonder, from report. My lord,
    The court of England emulates your merit   110
    And covets to embrace 'ee.
DALIELL.   I must wait on
    The princess in her fortunes.
OXFORD.   Will you please,
    Great lady, to set forward?
KATHERINE.   Being driven
    By fate, it were in vain to strive with heaven.   *Exeunt omnes.*

[V.ii]
    Enter King Henry, Surrey, Urswick, *and a guard of soldiers.*

KING HENRY.
    The counterfeit, King Perkin, is escap'd;
    Escape, so let him! He is hedg'd too fast
    Within the circuit of our English pale
    To steal out of our ports or leap the walls
    Which guard our land; the seas are rough and wider   5
    Than his weak arms can tug with. —Surrey, henceforth
    Your king may reign in quiet; turmoils past,
    Like some unquiet dream, have rather busied
    Our fancy than affrighted rest of state.

---

103. *fame*] public report.
103. *bravely spoken*] spoken well of.
[V.ii]
  3. *pale*] fence, enclosure.

But Surrey, why in articling a peace   10
With James of Scotland was not restitution
Of losses, which our subjects did sustain
By the Scotch inroads, questioned?

SURREY.   Both demanded
And urg'd, my lord, to which the king replied
In modest merriment, but smiling earnest,   15
How that our master Henry was much abler
To bear the detriments than he repay them.

KING HENRY.
The young man, I believe, spake honest truth;
'A studies to be wise betimes. —Has, Urswick,
Sir Rice ap Thomas and Lord Brooke our steward   20
Return'd the western gentlemen full thanks
From us for their tried loyalties?

URSWICK.   They have;
Which as if health and life had reign'd amongst 'em,
With open hearts they joyfully receiv'd.

KING HENRY.
Young Buckingham is a fair-natur'd prince,   25
Lovely in hopes and worthy of his father;

22. S.P. URSWICK.] *Weber; speech
assigned to Surrey in* Q.

10–17. *But . . . them*] "The Bishop [of Durham] also according to
another article of his instructions, demanded restitution of the spoils
taken by the Scottish, or damages for the same. But the Scottish com-
missioners answered . . . that the King's [Henry's] people were better able
to bear the loss than their master to repair it" (Bacon, XI, 279–280).

17. *detriments*] damages.

19. *betimes*] early.

20. *Sir . . . Brooke*] Both are mentioned by Bacon, but for a different
reason: "He sent the Lord Chamberlain, and the Lord Brooke, and Sir
Rice ap Thomas, with expedite forces to speed to Exeter to the rescue of the
town" (XI, 287).

25–28. *Buckingham . . . name*] "But first he [Henry] welcomed Edward,
Duke of Buckingham, a young noble, and well regarded Prince, in whose
Company came along a hundred Knights and Esquires of special Name"
(Gainsford, p. 203).

26. *Lovely . . . hopes*] of great promise.

26. *worthy . . . father*] Henry Stafford, Duke of Buckingham, had been
executed in 1483 by Richard III for attempting a revolt on behalf of Henry
(then the Earl of Richmond).

Attended by an hundred knights and squires
Of special name, he tender'd humble service,
Which we must ne'er forget. And Devonshire's wounds,
Though slight, shall find sound cure in our respect.   30

Enter Dawbney, *with* [*a guard, conducting*] Warbeck, Heron, John a
Water, Astley, Sketon.

DAWBNEY.
Life to the king, and safety fix his throne!
I here present you, royal sir, a shadow
Of majesty, but in effect a substance
Of pity; a young man in nothing grown
To ripeness but th' ambition of your mercy: 35
Perkin, the Christian world's strange wonder.

KING HENRY.   Dawbney,
We observe no wonder. I behold, 'tis true,
An ornament of nature, fine and polish'd,
A handsome youth indeed, but not admire him.
How came he to thy hands?

DAWBNEY.   From sanctuary   40
At Bewley, near Southampton, register'd
With these few followers for persons privileg'd.

KING HENRY.
I must not thank you, sir! You were to blame
To infringe the liberty of houses sacred.
Dare we be irreligious?

DAWBNEY.   Gracious lord,   45
They voluntarily resign'd themselves
Without compulsion.

KING HENRY.   So? 'Twas very well;
'Twas very, very well. —Turn now thine eyes,

---

28. *special*] distinguished, notable.
29. *Devonshire's wounds*] Gainsford states (p. 203) that Devonshire was
wounded in the arm by an arrow.
30. *respect*] favor.
31. *fix*] make secure.
35. *ambition of*] hope for.
39. *admire*] wonder at.
40–42. *From . . . privileg'd*] A sanctuary was a sacred place where fugitives
were immune from arrest. Warbeck had fled to "a Sanctuary town besides
Southampton, called Bewdley, where he, John Heron, Thomas a Water,
and others, registered themselves as Persons privileged" (Gainsford, p. 204).

Young man, upon thyself and thy past actions.
What revels in combustion through our kingdom   50
A frenzy of aspiring youth hath danc'd
Till, wanting breath, thy feet of pride have slipp'd
To break thy neck.
WARBECK.   But not my heart; my heart
Will mount till every drop of blood be frozen
By death's perpetual winter. If the sun   55
Of majesty be darken'd, let the sun
Of life be hid from me in an eclipse
Lasting and universal. Sir, remember
There was a shooting in of light when Richmond,
Not aiming at a crown, retir'd, and gladly,   60
For comfort, to the Duke of Bretaine's court.
Richard who swayed the scepter was reputed
A tyrant then; yet then a dawning glimmer'd
To some few wand'ring remnants, promising day
When first they ventur'd on a frightful shore   65
At Milford Haven—
DAWBNEY.   Whither speeds his boldness?
Check his rude tongue, great sir.
KING HENRY.   Oh let him range.
The player's on the stage still, 'tis his part;
'A does but act. —What followed?
WARBECK.   Bosworth Field,
Where at an instant, to the world's amazement,   70

---

61. Bretaine's] *Weber; Britaines Q.*

50. *combustion*] commotion.
59. *Richmond*] Henry VII was Earl of Richmond before he became king
by defeating Richard III at Bosworth Field (l. 69) after having landed at
Milford Haven (l. 66).
60–61. *retir'd . . . court*] Richmond twice retired to the court of Francis,
Duke of Brittany: in 1471 (Edward IV having regained the throne from
Henry VI), when Jasper Tudor, his uncle, took him there for political
asylum; and in 1483, when he returned there after an unsuccessful attempt
to invade England and overthrow Richard III. Ford probably is alluding
to the second incident.
66. *Milford Haven*] a harbor in south Wales, where Richmond landed to
invade England.
69. *Bosworth Field*] where Richmond defeated Richard III; located
twelve miles west of Leicester.

A morn to Richmond and a night to Richard
Appear'd at once. The tale is soon applied:
Fate, which crown'd these attempts when least assur'd,
Might have befriended others like resolv'd.

KING HENRY.

A pretty gallant! Thus your aunt of Burgundy,   75
Your duchess-aunt, inform'd her nephew; so
The lesson, prompted and well conn'd, was molded
Into familiar dialogue, oft rehearsed
Till, learnt by heart, 'tis now receiv'd for truth.

WARBECK.

Truth in her pure simplicity wants art   80
To put a feigned blush on. Scorn wears only
Such fashion as commends to gazers' eyes
Sad ulcerated novelty, far beneath
The sphere of majesty. In such a court,
Wisdom and gravity are proper robes,   85
By which the sovereign is best distinguish'd
From zanies to his greatness.

KING HENRY.   Sirrah, shift
Your antic pageantry and now appear
In your own nature, or you'll taste the danger
Of fooling out of season.

WARBECK.   I expect   90
No less than what severity calls justice,
And politicians safety. Let such beg
As feed on alms, but if there can be mercy
In a protested enemy, then may it
Descend to these poor creatures, whose engagements   95
To th' bettering of their fortunes have incurr'd
A loss of all; to them if any charity
Flow from some noble orator, in death
I owe the fee of thankfulness.

KING HENRY.   So brave!
What a bold knave is this!—Which of these rebels   100
Has been the Mayor of Cork?

---

83. *ulcerated*] having ulcers, irritated, poisoned.
87. *zanies*] clownish imitators.
94. *protested*] declared.

DAWBNEY.   This wise formality.—
Kneel to the king, 'ee rascals!
KING HENRY.   Canst thou hope
A pardon, where thy guilt is so apparent?
MAYOR OF CORK.
Under your good favors, as men are men, they may err; for
I confess, respectively, in taking great parts, the one side   105
prevailing, the other side must go down. Herein the point is
clear (if the proverb hold that "hanging goes by destiny")
that it is to little purpose to say this thing or that shall be
thus or thus; for as the fates will have it, so it must be, and
who can help it?   110
DAWBNEY.
Oh blockhead! Thou a privy-counselor?
Beg life, and cry aloud, "Heaven save King Henry!"
MAYOR OF CORK.
Every man knows what is best as it happens. For my own
part, I believe it is true, if I be not deceived, that kings must
be kings and subjects subjects. But which is which, you shall 115
pardon me for that. Whether we speak or hold our peace, all
are mortal; no man knows his end.
KING HENRY.
We trifle time with follies.
OMNES.   Mercy, mercy!
KING HENRY.
Urswick, command the dukeling and these fellows
To Digby, the lieutenant of the Tower.   120
With safety let them be convey'd to London.
It is our pleasure no uncivil outrage,
Taunts, or abuse be suffer'd to their persons.
They shall meet fairer law than they deserve.
Time may restore their wits, whom vain ambition   125
Hath many years distracted.
WARBECK.   Noble thoughts
Meet freedom in captivity. The Tower?
Our childhood's dreadful nursery.
KING HENRY.   No more.

---

101. *formality*] "that which pertains to outward form; also, an outward
appearance or semblance" (*OED*).
107. *hanging . . . destiny*] proverbial. Cf. Tilley, W 232.

URSWICK.

    Come, come, you shall have leisure to bethink 'ee.

                Exit Urswick *with* Perkin *and his* [*followers*].

KING HENRY.

    Was ever so much impudence in forgery?   130

    The custom, sure, of being styl'd a king

    Hath fasten'd in his thought that he is such,

    But we shall teach the lad another language.

    'Tis good we have him fast.

DAWBNEY.   The hangman's physic

    Will purge this saucy humor.

KING HENRY.   Very likely.   135

    Yet we could temper mercy with extremity,

    Being not too far provok'd.

Enter Oxford, Katherine *in her richest attire*, [Daliell,] *Jane, and attendants.*

OXFORD.   Great sir, be pleas'd

    With your accustomed grace to entertain

    The Princess Katherine Gordon.

KING HENRY.   Oxford, herein

    We must beshrew thy knowledge of our nature.   140

    A lady of her birth and virtues could not

    Have found us so unfurnish'd of good manners

    As not, on notice given, to have met her

    Halfway in point of love. —Excuse, fair cousin,

    The oversight. Oh fie, you may not kneel;   145

    'Tis most unfitting. First, vouchsafe this welcome,

    A welcome to your own, for you shall find us

    But guardian to your fortune and your honors.

KATHERINE.

    My fortunes and mine honors are weak champions,

    As both are now befriended, sir. However,   150

    Both bow before your clemency.

KING HENRY.   Our arms

    Shall circle them from malice. —A sweet lady!

    131–132. *The . . . such*] "Nay himself with long and continual counter-feiting and with often telling a lie, was turned (by habit) almost into the thing he seemed to be, and from a liar to a believer" (Bacon, XI, 210–211).

    136. *temper . . . extremity*] mix, or blend, mercy and severity.

    140. *beshrew*] blame.

Beauty incomparable! Here lives majesty
At league with love.

KATHERINE.   Oh sir, I have a husband.

KING HENRY.

We'll prove your father, husband, friend, and servant,   155
Prove what you wish to grant us. —Lords, be careful
A patent presently be drawn for issuing
A thousand pounds from our exchequer yearly
During our cousin's life. —Our queen shall be
Your chief companion, our own court your home,   160
Our subjects all your servants.

KATHERINE.   But my husband?

KING HENRY [to Daliell].

By all descriptions you are noble Daliell,
Whose generous truth hath fam'd a rare observance.
We thank 'ee; 'tis a goodness gives addition
To every title boasted from your ancestry,   165
In all most worthy.

DALIELL.   Worthier than your praises,
Right princely sir, I need not glory in.

KING HENRY.

Embrace him, lords. —[To Katherine.] Whoever calls you
  mistress
Is lifted in our charge. —A goodlier beauty
Mine eyes yet ne'er encounter'd.

KATHERINE.   Cruel misery   170
Of fate, what rests to hope for?

KING HENRY.   Forward, lords,
To London. —Fair, ere long I shall present 'ee
With a glad object, peace, and Huntley's blessing.

                                        Exeunt omnes.

[V.iii]
Enter Constable *and officers*, Warbeck, Urswick, *and* Lambert Simnel
like a falconer [, *followed by a mob*]. *A pair of stocks.*

CONSTABLE.

Make room there! Keep off, I require 'ee, and none come

---

163. *fam'd*] made famous.
163. *observance*] devotion (to the service of Katherine).
169. *charge*] care.
171. *rests*] remains.

within twelve foot of his majesty's new stocks, upon pain of
displeasure. —Bring forward the malefactors. —Friend,
you must to this gear, no remedy. —Open the hole, and in
with his legs, just in the middle hole; there, that hole.   5
—[Warbeck *is put in the stocks.*] Keep off, or I'll commit
you all. Shall not a man in authority be obeyed?—So, so,
there, 'tis as it should be. Put on the padlock and give me
the key. —Off, I say, keep off!

URSWICK.

Yet, Warbeck, clear thy conscience. Thou hast tasted   10
King Henry's mercy liberally. The law
Has forfeited thy life, an equal jury
Have doom'd thee to the gallows; twice, most wickedly,
Most desperately, hast thou escap'd the Tower,
Inveigling to thy party with thy witchcraft   15
Young Edward, Earl of Warwick, son to Clarence,
Whose head must pay the price of that attempt.
Poor gentleman, unhappy in his fate,
And ruin'd by thy cunning! So a mongrel
May pluck the true stag down. Yet, yet confess   20
Thy parentage, for yet the king has mercy.

SIMNEL.

You would be Dick the Fourth, very likely!
Your pedigree is publish'd. You are known
For Osbeck's son of Tournay, a loose runagate,
A landloper. Your father was a Jew,   25
Turn'd Christian merely to repair his miseries.
Where's now your kingship?

WARBECK.   Baited to my death?
Intolerable cruelty! I laugh at

---

4. *gear*] device.
12. *equal*] impartial, fair.
13–14. *twice ... Tower*] According to both Bacon (XI, 301–303) and
Gainsford (pp. 207–209), Warbeck twice plotted to escape, but succeeded
only the first time, gaining sanctuary at the Priory of Shyne, whence the
Prior returned him to Henry, requesting that Warbeck's life be spared; the
king had Warbeck set in the stocks at Westminster and Cheapside, and at
both places Warbeck read his confession. The second plot, which involved
the Earl of Warwick, was discovered before it could be executed, and the
two prisoners were sentenced to death.
25. *landloper*] vagabond.

The Duke of Richmond's practice on my fortunes.
Possession of a crown ne'er wanted heralds.   30

SIMNEL.
You will not know who I am?

URSWICK.   Lambert Simnel,
Your predecessor in a dangerous uproar;
But on submission, not alone receiv'd
To grace, but by the king vouchsaf'd his service.

SIMNEL.
I would be Earl of Warwick, toil'd and ruffled   35
Against my master, leap'd to catch the moon,
Vaunted my name Plantagenet, as you do:
An earl, forsooth, whenas in truth I was,
As you are, a mere rascal. Yet his majesty
(A prince compos'd of sweetness, heaven protect him)   40
Forgave me all my villainies, repriev'd
The sentence of a shameful end, admitted
My surety of obedience to his service;
And I am now his falconer, live plenteously,
Eat from the king's purse, and enjoy the sweetness   45
Of liberty and favor, sleep securely.
And is not this now better than to buffet
The hangman's clutches, or to brave the cordage
Of a tough halter which will break your neck?
So, then, the gallant totters! Prithee, Perkin,   50
Let my example lead thee. Be no longer
A counterfeit; confess, and hope for pardon.

WARBECK.
For pardon? Hold, my heartstrings, whiles contempt
Of injuries in scorn may bid defiance
To this base man's foul language. —Thou poor vermin,   55
How dar'st thou creep so near me? Thou an earl?
Why, thou enjoy'st as much of happiness
As all the swinge of slight ambition flew at.

---

35. *ruffled*] contended, struggled.
42–43. *admitted . . . surety*] accepted my pledge.
47–48. *buffet . . . clutches*] beat back the hangman's hands.
50. *totters*] one meaning of the word was "to swing from the gallows, to be hanged" (*OED*).
58. *swinge*] sway, control.

A dunghill was thy cradle. So a puddle
By virtue of the sunbeams breathes a vapor   60
To infect the purer air, which drops again
Into the muddy womb that first exhal'd it.
Bread and a slavish ease, with some assurance
From the base beadle's whip, crown'd all thy hopes.
But, sirrah, ran there in thy veins one drop   65
Of such a royal blood as flows in mine,
Thou wouldst not change condition to be second
In England's state without the crown itself.
Coarse creatures are incapable of excellence.
But let the world, as all to whom I am   70
This day a spectacle, to time deliver,
And by tradition fix posterity
Without another chronicle than truth,
How constantly my resolution suffer'd
A martyrdom of majesty.

SIMNEL.   He's past   75
Recovery; a Bedlam cannot cure him.

URSWICK.
Away, inform the king of his behavior.

SIMNEL.
Perkin, beware the rope. The hangman's coming.

URSWICK.
If yet thou hast no pity of thy body,
Pity thy soul!   *Exit* Simnel.

Enter Katherine, Jane, Daliell, *and* Oxford.

JANE.   Dear lady!
OXFORD.   Whither will 'ee,   80
Without respect of shame?
KATHERINE.   Forbear me, sir,
And trouble not the current of my duty.—
Oh my lov'd lord! Can any scorn be yours
In which I have no interest?—Some kind hand

---

63. *assurance*] protection.
64. *beadle*] an inferior officer of justice, one of whose duties was to punish
petty offenders.
72. *fix*] establish (for).
81. *Forbear me*] leave me alone.

Lend me assistance, that I may partake   85
Th' infliction of this penance. —My life's dearest,
Forgive me. I have stay'd too long from tend'ring
Attendance on reproach, yet bid me welcome.

WARBECK.

    Great miracle of constancy! My miseries
Were never bankrout of their confidence   90
In worst afflictions, till this. Now I feel them.
Report and thy deserts, thou best of creatures,
Might to eternity have stood a pattern
For every virtuous wife without this conquest.
Thou hast outdone belief, yet may their ruin   95
In after-marriages be never pitied
To whom thy story shall appear a fable.
Why wouldst thou prove so much unkind to greatness,
To glorify thy vows by such a servitude?
I cannot weep, but trust me, dear, my heart   100
Is liberal of passion. —Harry Richmond,
A woman's faith hath robb'd thy fame of triumph!

OXFORD.

    Sirrah, leave off your juggling, and tie up
The devil that ranges in your tongue.

URSWICK.   Thus witches,
Possess'd, even to their deaths deluded, say   105
They have been wolves and dogs, and sail'd in eggshells
Over the sea, and rid on fiery dragons,
Pass'd in the air more than a thousand miles
All in a night. The enemy of mankind
Is powerful, but false, and falsehood confident.   110

OXFORD.

    Remember, lady, who you are; come from
That impudent impostor.

KATHERINE.   You abuse us:
For when the holy churchman join'd our hands,
Our vows were real then; the ceremony
Was not in apparition, but in act.—   115

105. to] *Gifford; not in Q.*

---

103. *juggling*] deception.
115. *not . . . act*] not an illusion, but actuality.

Be what these people term thee, I am certain
Thou art my husband. No divorce in heaven
Has been sued out between us; 'tis injustice
For any earthly power to divide us.
Or we will live or let us die together.   120
There is a cruel mercy.

WARBECK.   Spite of tyranny
We reign in our affections, blessed woman!
Read in my destiny the wrack of honor;
Point out, in my contempt of death, to memory
Some miserable happiness, since herein,   125
Even when I fell, I stood enthron'd a monarch
Of one chaste wife's troth, pure and uncorrupted.
Fair angel of perfection, immortality
Shall raise thy name up to an adoration,
Court every rich opinion of true merit,   130
And saint it in the calendar of virtue,
When I am turn'd into the selfsame dust
Of which I was first form'd.

OXFORD.   The Lord Ambassador
Huntley, your father, madam, should 'a look on
Your strange subjection in a gaze so public, 135
Would blush on your behalf and wish his country
Unleft for entertainment to such sorrow.

KATHERINE.
Why art thou angry, Oxford? I must be
More peremptory in my duty. —Sir,
Impute it not unto immodesty   140
That I presume to press you to a legacy
Before we part forever.

WARBECK.   Let it be then
My heart, the rich remains of all my fortunes.

KATHERINE.
Confirm it with a kiss, pray.

WARBECK.   Oh with that

---

123. *wrack*] persecution.
129. *raise . . . adoration*] make you an object of worship.
131. *saint . . . calendar*] "The church calendar gave a list of canonized saints, the days dedicated to the memory of saints being registered" (Struble).

I wish to breathe my last. Upon thy lips,   145
Those equal twins of comeliness, I seal
The testament of honorable vows.
Whoever be that man that shall unkiss
This sacred print next, may he prove more thrifty
In this world's just applause, not more desertful.   150

KATHERINE.
By this sweet pledge of both our souls, I swear
To die a faithful widow to thy bed,
Not to be forc'd or won. Oh never, never!

    Enter Surrey, Dawbney, Huntley, *and* Crawford.

DAWBNEY.
Free the condemned person, quickly free him.
What has 'a yet confess'd?
URSWICK.   Nothing to purpose;   155
But still 'a will be king.
SURREY.   Prepare your journey
To a new kingdom then. —Unhappy madam,
Willfully foolish!—See, my Lord Ambassador,
Your lady daughter will not leave the counterfeit
In this disgrace of fate.
HUNTLEY.   I never pointed   160
Thy marriage, girl, but yet, being married,
Enjoy thy duty to a husband freely.
The griefs are mine. I glory in thy constancy
And must not say I wish that I had miss'd
Some partage in these trials of a patience.   165

KATHERINE.
You will forgive me, noble sir?
HUNTLEY.   Yes, yes;
In every duty of a wife and daughter
I dare not disavow thee. To your husband—
For such you are, sir—I impart a farewell
Of manly pity. —What your life has pass'd through,   170
The dangers of your end will make apparent.
And I can add, for comfort to your sufferance,
No cordial but the wonder of your frailty,
Which keeps so firm a station. We are parted.

---

149. *thrifty*] prosperous.   160. *pointed*] appointed.

WARBECK.

We are. A crown of peace renew thy age,   175
Most honorable Huntley. —Worthy Crawford,
We may embrace. I never thought thee injury.

CRAWFORD.

Nor was I ever guilty of neglect
Which might procure such thought. I take my leave, sir.

WARBECK.

To you, Lord Daliell—what? Accept a sigh;   180
'Tis hearty and in earnest.

DALIELL.   I want utterance;
My silence is my farewell.

KATHERINE.   Oh, oh—

JANE.   Sweet madam,
What do you mean?—[*To* Daliell.]   My lord, your hand.

DALIELL.   Dear lady,
Be pleas'd that I may wait 'ee to your lodging.

                            Exeunt Daliell, Katherine, Jane.

*Enter Sheriff and officers; Sketon, Astley, Heron, and Mayor with halters
about their necks.*

OXFORD.

Look 'ee, behold your followers, appointed   185
To wait on 'ee in death.

WARBECK.   Why, peers of England,
We'll lead 'em on courageously. I read
A triumph over tyranny upon
Their several foreheads. —Faint not in the moment
Of victory! Our ends, and Warwick's head,   190
Innocent Warwick's head (for we are prologue
But to his tragedy), conclude the wonder
Of Henry's fears; and then the glorious race
Of fourteen kings Plantagenets determines
In this last issue male. Heaven be obey'd.   195
Impoverish time of its amazement, friends,

190–195. *Our . . . male*] "This was also the end not only of this noble and
commiserable person Edward the Earl of Warwick . . . but likewise of the
line-male of the Plantagenets, which had flourished in great royalty and
renown from the time of . . . King Henry the Second" (Bacon, XI, 305).

194. *determines*] terminates.

And we will prove as trusty in our payments,
As prodigal to nature in our debts.
Death? Pish, 'tis but a sound, a name of air,
A minute's storm, or not so much. To tumble   200
From bed to bed, be massacred alive
By some physicians for a month or two,
In hope of freedom from a fever's torments,
Might stagger manhood; here, the pain is past
Ere sensibly 'tis felt. Be men of spirit!   205
Spurn coward passion! So illustrious mention
Shall blaze our names, and style us kings o'er death.

DAWBNEY.
Away, impostor beyond precedent!

                        Exeunt all officers and prisoners.

No chronicle records his fellow.

HUNTLEY.   I have
Not thoughts left. 'Tis sufficient in such cases   210
Just laws ought to proceed.

        Enter King Henry, Durham, *and Hialas.*

KING HENRY.   We are resolv'd.
Your business, noble lords, shall find success
Such as your king importunes.

HUNTLEY.   You are gracious.

KING HENRY.
Perkin, we are inform'd, is arm'd to die.
In that we'll honor him. Our lords shall follow   215
To see the execution. And from hence
We gather this fit use: that "public states,
As our particular bodies, taste most good
In health when purged of corrupted blood."   *Exeunt omnes.*

FINIS.

---

217. *gather . . . use*] draw this practical application.
218. *taste*] feel.

EPILOGUE

Here has appear'd, though in a several fashion,
The threats of majesty, the strength of passion,
Hopes of an empire, change of fortunes—all
What can to theaters of greatness fall,
Proving their weak foundations. Who will please,   5
Amongst such several sights, to censure these
No births abortive, nor a bastard brood
(Shame to a parentage or fosterhood),
May warrant by their loves all just excuses,
And often find a welcome to the Muses.   10

FINIS.

1. *several*] diverse.
6. *censure these*] judge these (to be).
9. *warrant*] sanction.

Appendix

Chronology

Approximate years are indicated by *, occurrences in doubt by (?).

Political and Literary Events	Life and Major Works of John Ford

1558
Accession of Queen Elizabeth.
Robert Greene born.
Thomas Kyd born.

1560
George Chapman born.

1561
Francis Bacon born.

1564
Shakespeare born.
Christopher Marlowe born.

1570
Thomas Heywood born.*

1572
Thomas Dekker born.*
John Donne born.
Massacre of St. Bartholomew's Day.

1573
Ben Jonson born.

1576
The Theatre, the first permanent public theater in London, established by James Burbage.
John Marston born.

1577
The Curtain theater opened.
Holinshed's *Chronicles of England, Scotland and Ireland.*
Drake begins circumnavigation of the earth; completed 1580.

1578
John Lyly's *Euphues: The Anatomy of Wit.*

1579
John Fletcher born.
Sir Thomas North's translation of Plutarch's *Lives.*

1580
Thomas Middleton born.

1583
Philip Massinger born.

1584
Francis Beaumont born.*

1586
Death of Sir Philip Sidney.

John Ford born at Islington, Devonshire, April 17.

1587
The Rose theater opened by Henslowe.
Marlowe's *TAMBURLAINE*, Part I.*
Execution of Mary, Queen of Scots.
Drake raids Cadiz.

1588
Defeat of the Spanish Armada.
Marlowe's *TAMBURLAINE*, Part II.*

1589
Greene's *FRIAR BACON AND FRIAR BUNGAY.*
Marlowe's *THE JEW OF MALTA.*
Kyd's *THE SPANISH TRAGEDY.*

1590
Spenser's *Faerie Queene* (Books I–III) published.
Sidney's *Arcadia* published.
Shakespeare's *HENRY VI*, Parts I–III,* *TITUS ANDRONICUS.*

1591
Shakespeare's *RICHARD III.*

1592
Marlowe's *DOCTOR FAUSTUS**
and *EDWARD II.**
Shakespeare's *TAMING OF THE
SHREW** and *THE COMEDY OF
ERRORS.**
Death of Greene.

1593
Shakespeare's *LOVE'S LABOR'S
LOST;* Venus and Adonis* published.
Death of Marlowe.
Theaters closed on account of
plague.

1594
Shakespeare's *TWO GENTLE-
MEN OF VERONA;* The Rape of
Lucrece* published.
Shakespeare's company becomes
Lord Chamberlain's Men.
Death of Kyd.

1595
The Swan theater built.
Sidney's *Defense of Poesy* published.
Shakespeare's *ROMEO AND
JULIET,* A MIDSUMMER
NIGHT'S DREAM,* RICHARD
II.**
Raleigh's first expedition to Guiana.

1596
Spenser's *Faerie Queene* (Books IV–
VI) published.
Shakespeare's *MERCHANT OF
VENICE,* KING JOHN.**
James Shirley born.

1597
Bacon's *Essays* (first edition).
Shakespeare's *HENRY IV*, Part I.*

1598
Demolition of The Theatre.
Shakespeare's *MUCH ADO
ABOUT NOTHING,* HENRY IV*,
Part II.*

Jonson's *EVERY MAN IN HIS HUMOR* (first version).

Seven books of Chapman's translation of Homer's *Iliad* published.

1599

The Paul's Boys reopen their theater.

The Globe theater opened.

Shakespeare's *AS YOU LIKE IT*,* *HENRY V, JULIUS CAESAR.*

Marston's *ANTONIO AND MELLIDA*,* Parts I and II.

Dekker's *THE SHOEMAKERS' HOLIDAY.*

Death of Spenser.

1600

Shakespeare's *TWELFTH NIGHT.*

The Fortune theater built by Alleyn.

The Children of the Chapel begin to play at the Blackfriars.

1601

Shakespeare's *HAMLET*,* *MERRY WIVES OF WINDSOR.*

Insurrection and execution of the Earl of Essex.

Jonson's *POETASTER* (ridiculing Marston).

Brief residence at Oxford (?).

1602

Shakespeare's *TROILUS AND CRESSIDA.*

Admitted to the Middle Temple, November 16.

1603

Death of Queen Elizabeth; accession of James VI of Scotland as James I.

Florio's translation of Montaigne's *Essays* published.

Shakespeare's *ALL'S WELL THAT ENDS WELL.*

Heywood's *A WOMAN KILLED WITH KINDNESS.*

Marston's *THE MALCONTENT.*

Shakespeare's company becomes the King's Men.

1604

Shakespeare's *MEASURE FOR MEASURE,** *OTHELLO.**
Marston's *THE FAWN.**
Chapman's *BUSSY D'AMBOIS.**

1605

Shakespeare's *KING LEAR.**
Marston's *THE DUTCH COURTESAN.**
Bacon's *Advancement of Learning* published.
The Gunpowder Plot.

Expelled from the Middle Temple for not paying buttery bill.

1606

Shakespeare's *MACBETH.**
Jonson's *VOLPONE.**
Tourneur's *REVENGER'S TRAGEDY.**
The Red Bull theater built.
Death of John Lyly.

Publication of *Fame's Memorial* (poem) and *Honor Triumphant* (pamphlet).
Barnes's *Four Books of Offices*, with commendatory verses by Ford, and Cooper's *Funeral Tears for the Death of the Earl of Devonshire*, with a poem by Ford, published.

1607

Shakespeare's *ANTONY AND CLEOPATRA.**
Beaumont's *KNIGHT OF THE BURNING PESTLE.**
Settlement of Jamestown, Virginia.

1608

Shakespeare's *CORIOLANUS,** *TIMON OF ATHENS,** *PERICLES.**
Chapman's *CONSPIRACY AND TRAGEDY OF CHARLES, DUKE OF BYRON.**
Dekker's *Gull's Hornbook* published.
Richard Burbage leases Blackfriars Theatre for King's Company.
John Milton born.

Reinstated at the Middle Temple, June 10.

1609

Shakespeare's *CYMBELINE;**
Sonnets published.
Jonson's *EPICOENE.*

1610
Jonson's *ALCHEMIST.*
Chapman's *REVENGE OF BUSSY D'AMBOIS.**
Richard Crashaw born.

Receives total bequest of £10 upon the death of his father, Thomas Ford.

1611
Authorized (King James) Version of the Bible published.
Shakespeare's *THE WINTER'S TALE,** *THE TEMPEST.**
Beaumont and Fletcher's *A KING AND NO KING.*
Tourneur's *ATHEIST'S TRAGEDY.**
Middleton's *A CHASTE MAID IN CHEAPSIDE.*
Chapman's translation of *Iliad* completed.

1612
Webster's *THE WHITE DEVIL.**

1613
The Globe theater burned.
Shakespeare's *HENRY VIII* (with Fletcher).
Webster's *THE DUCHESS OF MALFI.**
Sir Thomas Overbury murdered.

Christ's Bloody Sweat (poem) and *The Golden Mean* (pamphlet) published.

1614
The Globe theater rebuilt.
The Hope Theatre built.
Jonson's *BARTHOLOMEW FAIR.*

1615

Sir Thomas Overbury's Ghost (book; not extant) entered in the Stationers' Register, November 25.

1616
Publication of Folio edition of Jonson's *WORKS.*
Chapman's *Whole Works of Homer.*
Death of Shakespeare.
Death of Beaumont.

Granted £20 per year by will of his older brother, Henry, September 17.

1617

One of forty members of the Middle Temple admonished for wearing hats instead of lawyers' caps.

1618
Outbreak of Thirty Years War.
Execution of Raleigh.

1620
Pilgrim Fathers land at Plymouth.

A Line of Life (pamphlet) published.

1621
Middleton's *WOMEN BEWARE WOMEN.**
Robert Burton's *Anatomy of Melancholy* published.
Andrew Marvell born.

THE WITCH OF EDMONTON, with Dekker and Rowley.

1622
Middleton and Rowley's *THE CHANGELING.**
Henry Vaughan born.

1623
Publication of Folio edition of Shakespeare's *COMEDIES, HISTORIES, AND TRAGEDIES.*

THE SPANISH GYPSY (?), with Middleton and Rowley (Lady Elizabeth's company).
Webster's *THE DUCHESS OF MALFI* and Cockeram's *The English Dictionary*, both with commendatory verses by Ford, published.

1624

THE SUN'S DARLING, with Dekker, licensed by Herbert.
THE BRISTOW MERCHANT (lost) and *THE FAIRY KNIGHT* (lost [?]), both with Dekker.
THE LATE MURDER OF THE SON UPON THE MOTHER (lost), with Dekker, Rowley, and Webster.

1625
Death of King James I; accession of Charles I.
Death of Fletcher.

THE FAIR MAID OF THE INN, with Fletcher, Massinger, and Webster.

1626
Death of Tourneur.
Death of Bacon.

1627
Death of Middleton.

1628
Petition of Right.
Buckingham assassinated.

THE LOVER'S MELANCHOLY
(published 1629).

1629

Shirley's *THE WEDDING* and
Massinger's *THE ROMAN ACTOR*,
both with commendatory verses by
Ford, published.

1630

*BEAUTY IN A TRANCE** (lost).

1631
Shirley's *THE TRAITOR*.
Death of Donne.
John Dryden born.

1632
Massinger's *THE CITY MADAM*.*

Brome's *THE NORTHERN LASS*,
with commendatory verses by Ford,
published.

1633
Donne's *Poems* published.
Death of George Herbert.

*THE BROKEN HEART, LOVE'S
SACRIFICE*, and *'TIS PITY SHE'S
A WHORE* published.

1634
Death of Chapman, Marston, Web-
ster.*
Publication of *THE TWO NOBLE
KINSMEN*, with title-page attri-
bution to Shakespeare and Fletcher.
Milton's *Comus*.

PERKIN WARBECK published.

1635
Sir Thomas Browne's *Religio Medici*.

1636

Massinger's *THE GREAT DUKE
OF FLORENCE*, with commendatory verses by Ford, published.

1637
Death of Jonson.

1638

THE LADY'S TRIAL licensed.
THE FANCIES CHASTE AND NOBLE published.
Jonsonus Virbius, with commendatory verses by Ford, published.

1639
First Bishops' War.
Death of Carew.*

Publication of *THE LADY'S TRIAL*, with dedication signed by Ford.
No certain later record of Ford.

1640
Short Parliament.
Long Parliament impeaches Laud.
Death of Massinger, Burton.

1641
Irish rebel.
Death of Heywood.

1642
Charles I leaves London; Civil War breaks out.
Shirley's *COURT SECRET*.
All theaters closed by Act of Parliament.

1643
Parliament swears to the Solemn League and Covenant.

1645
Ordinance for New Model Army enacted.

1646
End of First Civil War.

1647
Army occupies London.
Charles I forms alliance with Scots.
Publication of Folio edition of Beaumont and Fletcher's *COMEDIES AND TRAGEDIES*.

1648
Second Civil War.

1649
Execution of Charles I.

1650
Jeremy Collier born.

1651
Hobbes' *Leviathan* published.

1652
First Dutch War began (ended 1654).
Thomas Otway born.

1653
Nathaniel Lee born.*   *THE QUEEN* published.

1656
D'Avenant's *THE SIEGE OF RHODES* performed at Rutland House.

1657
John Dennis born.

1658
Death of Oliver Cromwell.
D'Avenant's *THE CRUELTY OF THE SPANIARDS IN PERU* performed at the Cockpit.

Howard's *THE GREAT FAVORITE, OR THE DUKE OF LERMA*, possibly a rewriting of some earlier play by Ford, published.

1660
Restoration of Charles II.
Theatrical patents granted to Thomas Killigrew and Sir William D'Avenant, authorizing them to form, respectively, the King's and the Duke of York's Companies.

AN ILL BEGINNING HAS A GOOD END (lost), *THE LONDON MERCHANT* (lost), and *THE ROYAL COMBAT* (lost) all entered in the Stationers' Register and attributed to Ford by Moseley.